Benjamin Harrison

23rd President of the United States

Benjamin Harrison was the only President from Indiana. He was also the only grandson of a President to become President in his turn. (Library of Congress.)

Benjamin Harrison

23rd President of the United States

Rita Stevens

 **GARRETT EDUCATIONAL CORPORATION**

Manufactured in the United States of America

Edited and produced by Synthegraphics Corporation

Library of Congress Cataloging in Publication Data

Stevens, Rita.
  Benjamin Harrison, 23rd president of the United States.
  (Presidents of the United States)
  Bibliography: p.
  Includes index.
  Summary: A biography focusing on the military and political career of the only grandson of a president to become president himself.
  1. Harrison, Benjamin, 1833–1901 — Juvenile literature.
2. Presidents — United States — Biography — Juvenile literature. [1. Harrison, Benjamin, 1833–1901.
2. Presidents.] I. Title. II. Title: Benjamin Harrison, twenty-third president of the United States. III. Series.
E702.S74 1989   973.8'6'0924 — dc19 [B] [92]
88-24747
ISBN 0-944483-15-1

Contents

Chronology for Benjamin Harrison

1833   Born on August 20 in North Bend, Ohio

1847–
1852   Educated at Farmer's College in Cincinnati, Ohio, and at Miami University in Oxford, Ohio

1853   Married Caroline Lavinia Scott on October 19

1854   Admitted to the Ohio bar; moved to Indianapolis, Indiana

1856   Joined the Republican Party

1861–
1862   Served as reporter of the State Supreme Court of Indiana

1862–
1865   Served with the 70th Indiana Infantry Regiment in the Union Army during the Civil War, reaching rank of brigadier general

1881–
1887   Served as U.S. senator from Indiana

1888   Elected President on 100th anniversary of first presidential election

1892   Defeated by Grover Cleveland in attempt to be re-elected President

1896   Married Mary Lord Dimmick on April 6

1901   Died in Indianapolis on March 13

Chapter 1

The Campaign for Atlanta

In the spring of 1864, the American Civil War was three years old. When the first shots were fired in April 1861, the North, or Union, boasted confidently that it would defeat the South, or Confederacy, in less than three months. But as the months and then the years went by, neither side was able to gain a clear victory. Now it was May of 1864. Neither side yet knew it, but the end was in sight.

Near the Confederate capital of Richmond, Virginia, the Union commander, Ulysses S. Grant, was relentlessly pursuing the army of Robert E. Lee, the leader of the Confederate forces. And in the Deep South, in Georgia, Confederate General Joseph Johnston was under attack as well. In an attempt to smash Johnston's army, Union General William Tecumseh Sherman had led his forces into the heart of the South. Day by day, mile by mile, Sherman drove Johnston back toward Atlanta. Both generals knew that if the Union captured Atlanta, with its railroad lines that were desperately needed to carry food and military supplies through the struggling South, it would be a crippling blow to the Confederacy—perhaps a death blow.

THE BATTLE OF RESACA

On the evening of Friday, May 13, Johnston's forces were dug in behind defenses at the small Georgia town of Resaca, northwest of Atlanta. Johnston occupied a well-fortified position, one that would be easy to defend in case of attack. The Confederate leader was sure that if Sherman did attack, the Union losses would be heavy. He also was sure that the Confederacy would hold Resaca and continue to block Sherman's path to Atlanta.

That same evening, Sherman's forces were encamped outside Resaca. One division was led by Major General Joseph Hooker, called "Fighting Joe" by his men. One brigade in that division was commanded by General William T. Ward. And one regiment in that brigade was led by a 30-year-old lawyer from Indiana named Benjamin Harrison.

Short, slender, and soft spoken, Harrison was not a warrior by nature. "I am not a Julius Caesar, nor a Napoleon, but a plain Hoosier colonel, with no more relish for a fight than for a good breakfast . . . and hardly so much," he said. And although he bore the rank of colonel and had commanded the 70th Indiana Infantry Regiment for almost two years, Harrison had seen little actual combat. He and his men had engaged in a few minor skirmishes with rebel bands in Kentucky and Tennessee, but dawn would bring their first taste of pitched battle.

Night Thoughts

The letter Harrison wrote to his wife that night reveals much of his sensitive, affectionate, deeply religious character. "I must write you tonight as we look for battle tomorrow, and God only knows who shall come safely through it," he said, adding, "May God in His great mercy give us a great victory and may the nation give him the praise." Harrison went on to say, in his thoughtful, matter-of-fact way, "You will perhaps like to know how I feel on the eve of my first great battle. Well, I do not feel in the least excited, nor any sense of shrinking. I am in my usual good spirits, though not at all insensible to grave responsibilities and risks which I must bear tomorrow."

After urging his wife to remain brave and strong for their children's sake, Harrison ended the letter by saying, "Should I come alive through the fight to get home . . . I hope to see you all in good time." Then he blew out his candle, rolled up in his dusty blanket, and tried to snatch a few hours' much-needed sleep.

Confusion and Combat

When the battle started on May 14, Colonel Harrison was ordered to take his men and storm a hill overlooking the road to Resaca. Confederate sharpshooters manned the hilltop. The assignment was an extremely dangerous one. In order to reach the rebel position, Harrison and his men had to run down the side of the hill they occupied, struggle through a brushy pine thicket, run across a half-mile or so of open ground, and then scramble up the hill occupied by the Confederates. All this time they would be under deadly fire from enemy rifles above.

Harrison ordered his men to advance. However, upon reaching the bottom of the hill they occupied with some casualties, Harrison discovered, to his dismay, that General Ward had issued the wrong orders. The general now wanted Harrison to lead his regiment back *up* the hill they had just descended to the safety of the crest. Because climbing would be slow and the Confederate riflemen had already spotted the 70th, the retreat would be even more hazardous than the ini-

*Shouting "Come on, boys!" Colonel "Little Ben" Harrison led
his men in their first combat charge against the Confederate
troops of General J.B. Hood at the Battle of Resaca. (Library
of Congress.)*

tial advance had been. The furious Colonel Harrison lay pressed as flat to the ground as he could get, watching enemy bullets strike the sand just above his head and cursing Ward. Then he ordered his men to retreat one at a time or in small groups. By the end of the day, he had brought them all back to their original position, with no further casualties.

On the next day, the 15th, Harrison and his men were ordered to capture a cluster of enemy rifle pits (walled trenches from which Confederate soldiers could fire on advancing Union troops). Although weary, Harrison immediately led the 70th into position. Opposite them was a line of chest-high wooden walls behind which waited Confederate troops under the command of the famous General J.B. Hood.

Ignoring the murderous hail of bullets that swept through the 70th as soon as it left cover, Harrison led his men straight toward the enemy. One observer remembered seeing the little colonel "standing up there right in front of the rebels, waving his sword in one hand and brandishing a revolver in the other." Harrison later recalled, "I cheered the men forward and, with a wild yell, they [penetrated the wooden walls], striking down and bayoneting the gunners, many of whom defiantly stuck by their guns until struck down." It was Harrison's first experience of combat. It was not to be his last.

NEW HOPE CHURCH AND KENNESAW

Despite all Confederate efforts, Resaca fell to the Union that night. Johnston and his men were forced to retreat a little closer to Atlanta.

The next day, May 16th, the men of the 70th sadly returned to the battlefield at Resaca to bury their dead comrades and the Confederate soldiers they had killed. But the aftermath of battle also brought some cheer. Both Hooker and Sherman praised the valiant charge of the 70th and its leader, Colonel Benjamin Harrison. Because Ward had been seriously injured in the fighting, Harrison was asked to take temporary command of the brigade. Only two days before, Harrison had never faced enemy fire or led men under attack. Now he was commanding a whole brigade—one that would play an important part in the Atlanta campaign that helped end the war.

From May 26 to 28, Colonel Harrison's brigade fought a pitched battle with the Confederates at New Hope Church, Georgia. Because the Confederates had 16 cannon and 5,000 riflemen, Union losses were very heavy. Johnston later boasted that his forces turned the site into a "hell hole" for the Union. Several times Harrison led the 70th in daring charges to capture enemy positions. Finally, the Confederates retreated a few more miles toward Atlanta, the city that Confederate President Jefferson Davis had called "vital" to the survival of the Confederacy.

Field Surgeon

On June 15, Union and Confederate forces clashed again near Kennesaw Mountain, Georgia. Days later, after being ordered to lead the 70th against an enemy position, Harrison described the confrontation in a letter to Carrie, his wife:

> My Regiment was advanced without any support to within three hundred yards of a strong rebel [position]. . . . We stood there fighting an unseen foe for an hour and a half without flinching, while the enemy's shells and grapes [grapeshot, with which muskets were loaded] fell like hail in our ranks, tearing down large trees and filling the air with splinters. Two or three of my men had their heads torn off down close to the shoulders and others had fearful wounds.

Despite such horrors, the 70th held its ground, retreating under orders only after nightfall. But Harrison's duties were far from over. The regimental surgeons had somehow become separated from the troops. Because Harrison could not bear to see his wounded men suffering with no relief in sight, he rolled up his sleeves and did the best he could as an emergency surgeon. As he reported to Carrie:

> Poor Fellows! I was but an awkward surgeon, of course, but I hope I gave them some relief. There were some ghastly wounds. . . . I pulled out of one poor fellow's arm a splinter five or six inches long and as thick as my three fingers.

"Little Ben"

Harrison's bravery and his concern for his men helped forge a close bond between the 70th and its leader. The colonel wrote to Carrie, "I wouldn't like to leave my Regiment to the command of another in a fight. I have got to love them for their bravery and for dangers we have shared together. I have heard many similar expressions from the men towards me."

For their part, the men of the 70th affectionately called their tough leader "Little Ben," a nickname he bore proudly throughout the Atlanta campaign. In just one month, the mild-mannered Hoosier lawyer had grown tough indeed. He had led men into battle, taken over command for a fallen senior officer, buried his dead, and doctored his wounded.

The Atlanta campaign would include some of the fiercest fighting of the war. The Confederacy was struggling desperately, on its own soil, for its very life. Union General Sherman was a ruthless and destructive opponent, determined to crush the Confederacy and to "make old and young, rich and poor, feel the hard hand of war." Throughout June and July, in the blistering, sweltering heat of a Georgia summer, Sherman pushed closer and closer to his goal, driving the

Confederate troops back step by step. On July 7, Harrison wrote to Carrie that the Union forces were within 10 miles of their goal. "We can see the steeples of the churches in Atlanta," he said. The moment was at hand for the Union's final push and the Confederacy's final defense.

PEACHTREE CREEK

On July 20, Union forces crossed Peachtree Creek, a small stream about two miles north of Atlanta. Harrison and the 70th were among those ordered to make camp along the low-lying creek bed, shielded from enemy eyes by a low ridge. The men were cooking, sleeping, or mending their gear in the hastily constructed camp when disaster struck. General J.B. Hood, whom Harrison had already faced in battle and who had replaced Johnston as the Confederate commander, decided on a bold and risky surprise attack. He led his men in a wild charge at what he thought was a weak place in the Union line—the very place where Harrison's men and another brigade were camped.

Harrison did not hesitate. One soldier who was there said later, "Harrison put both spurs to his horse and dashed forward up the hill, in front of his brigade, and both brigades cheering ran rapidly . . . up the hill." The colonel issued only one command: to hold back the enemy with hand-to-hand fighting and, at all costs, to keep the Union line from breaking. It is said that he cried, "Come on, boys, we've never been licked yet, and we won't begin now. We haven't much ammunition, but if necessary we can give them the cold steel [bayonets], and before we get licked we will club them down, so come on!"

Hood's reckless attack failed. Harrison and his men managed to reach the top of the ridge and, in a wild tangle of firing, stabbing, and clubbing, drove the Confederate troops back down its far side. The Union line did not break. Many experts think that if it had, the Union Army might have been split in two and the Battle of Atlanta might have been won by the Confederacy. Thanks to Harrison's quick thinking and unquestioned courage, this did not happen. The Confederates fell back again, and the road to Atlanta was now open.

THE SIEGE

August was a long, hard month for Harrison. For two months he had been living on the knife-edge of nervous excitement, fighting battle after battle and proving his leadership and bravery every day. Now the fighting was over, at least for the moment. Atlanta was under siege. Sherman's forces had surrounded the city, cutting off supplies of food, fuel, and medicine. No one could enter or leave the once-prosperous city, where soldiers and citizens alike now lived in dread of the collapse that was certain to come. Everyone knew that it was only a matter of time until Sherman's army marched victorious through the streets of Atlanta.

In the meantime, Harrison reported to Carrie, "My life drags along very wearily now." He missed her and their two children, and he worried about her health, having heard that she was seriously ill in far-off Indianapolis, Indiana. Then, on August 20, his 31st birthday, Harrison received the happy news that she had recovered. Twelve days later, he had some happy news of his own to send her.

Flaming Atlanta

Atlanta fell to the Union forces on September 1, 1864. Confusion reigned as Sherman's men swarmed into the city, looting and setting fires, until before long Atlanta was in flames — and the hopes of the Confederacy with it. (The siege and fall of Atlanta are colorfully described from the southern point of view in the famous book and movie *Gone with the Wind*.) Among the first to enter the fallen city, right behind Sherman, was Colonel Benjamin Harrison. On September 2, he scribbled a note to Carrie, saying, "Atlanta is ours . . . and I send you a piece of cedar plucked from a door yard in Atlanta yesterday."

To Harrison, the end of the Atlanta campaign brought more than the joy of a Union victory and the pride a leader feels in men who have fought well under his command. It brought the welcome news that at last, after two years of field duty, he had leave to go home, to see his wife and children again. He left Atlanta a few days later.

Harrison had started the Atlanta campaign as an untried warrior. Now he was a respected and experienced military leader. He was even a hero of sorts—"the Hero of Peachtree Creek," many newspapers called him. And although he began the campaign as a colonel, he was not destined to remain one.

The day after the Battle of Peachtree Creek, "Fighting Joe" Hooker rode along the Union lines. Enthusiastically, he shook the hand of the modest colonel who had very likely saved the Union from a costly and embarrassing defeat. "Harrison, by God, I'll make you a brigadier for this fight," Hooker declared. Neither man knew it then, but Benjamin Harrison was to become much more than a brigadier general. Twenty-five years after the end of the Civil War, he became the 23rd President of the United States and the leader of an entire nation.

Chapter 2
A Heroic Heritage

To the many people who knew Benjamin Harrison, it came as no surprise that he ended the war as a hero, or that he later became President. Indeed, some of them expected no less. Harrison came from a family with a long and distinguished history of military and government service. Like many descendants of famous or successful families, he was expected to follow in his ancestors' footsteps.

Yet the children of famous parents often have both positive and negative feelings about their heritage. On one hand, they may be proud of their families' achievements and want to equal those achievements. On the other hand, however, they may wish to be judged on their own merits, rather than as the sons of daughters of famous people. Harrison felt these mixed feelings throughout his life. As a child, he heard family stories and legends about his famous great-grandfather, also named Benjamin, who had signed the Declaration of Independence, and his grandfather, William Henry Harrison, a famous fighter in the Northwest Territory. He was seven years old when his grandfather became the ninth President of the United States, and was known forever after as "the grandson of Old Tippecanoe." His father, John Scott Harrison, was a member of the U.S. House of Representatives. Harrison took great pride in this family heritage, which undoubtedly inspired him to seek a life of public service for himself.

However, Benjamin refused to be just another Harrison. Although proud of his family, he did not use his name or family fame to gain attention or glory for himself. Further, he refused to let others use his family name on his behalf. Early in his political career, when Harrison was a 23-year-old lawyer just starting to make a name for himself in the Republican Party, some party members insisted that he make a speech on behalf of the Republican presidential candidate, John C. Frémont. They introduced Benjamin to the waiting crowd as "the grandson of ex-President William Henry Harrison." The young speaker straightened his rumpled jacket and said firmly, "I want it understood that I am the grandson of nobody. I believe that every man should stand on his own merits." This independent, fair-minded philosophy stayed with Harrison throughout his career.

FAMILY HISTORY

The first of Harrison's ancestors in America was also named Benjamin Harrison. He was an Englishman who came to live in the Virginia colony in 1632, just 25 years after the founding of Jamestown, the first permanent settlement in North America. He was the first of five generations of Benjamin Harrisons who lived in Virginia until 1791. They were educated farmers who lived on a family estate called Berkeley in Charles City County, Virginia. Each new generation served in the local division of the militia (a volunteer defense force), on the local town council, and in the colony's governing body, which was called the House of Burgesses. In short, they were influential and well-respected colonial leaders.

The Signer

The fifth in the Virginia series of Benjamin Harrisons, President Benjamin Harrison's great-grandfather, was a famous figure within the family. He was something of a hero to young Ben, who took pleasure in their shared name. The Harrisons always called this ancestor "the Signer."

The Signer was born around 1726. He grew up on the family homestead and attended William and Mary College in Virginia, as did many other important colonial Americans, including Thomas Jefferson. Harrison served in the House of Burgesses. Then, during the exciting and difficult days that saw the birth of American democracy, he was sent as a delegate to the First and Second Continental Congresses. He was the chairman of the committee that debated—and eventually accepted—Jefferson's Declaration of Independence. And he proudly signed his name to that historic document, thus supplying his nickname.

After the United States won its independence from the British, Harrison's great-grandfather went on to serve as the speaker of Virginia's new legislative body, the House of Delegates. He also was elected governor of Virginia for three terms. But his third son, William Henry Harrison, the next member of the Harrison clan to win fame, achieved a higher position still.

Child of the Revolution

Born in 1773, William Henry Harrison was three years old when his father signed the Declaration of Independence. He was 10 when the British finally gave up their claim to their former North American colonies, 14 when the United States Constitution was adopted, and 16 when George Washington became the nation's first President. But it was not until his own inauguration as President in 1841 that William Henry Harrison received the nickname "Child of the Revolution."

Harrison had a colorful career before the presidency. He briefly studied medicine, then entered the army. He fought in the Indian wars in the Northwest Territories, chiefly in the area that is now Ohio. After leaving the army, he settled near Cincinnati, Ohio. It was William Henry Harrison who established a branch of the old Virginia family in the Midwest. And it was this Midwestern branch of the Harrison family that was to play an important part in American public life during the coming years.

William Henry Harrison served as secretary of the Northwest Territories and governor of the Indiana Territory. He then commanded American forces in important battles against the Shawnee Indians and the British. After the War of 1812, he was elected to the U.S. Senate in 1825, and then was appointed minister (a diplomatic post similar to that of an ambassador today) to the South American nation of Colombia. He was elected President in 1840, but his presidency was destined not to be as glorious as his military career. He died of pneumonia after one month in office.

BEN'S PARENTS

Benjamin's father, John Scott Harrison, was born in 1804, the fifth of William Henry Harrison's 10 children. As a young man, he began the study of law, but gave it up to manage his father's large farm and estate at North Bend, near Cincinnati, while William Henry Harrison was busy with his political career. In return, William Henry gave John Scott a 600-acre farm of his own. It was called the Point, because it occupied a long point of land where the Big Miami River flowed into the Ohio River. There John Scott Harrison lived

Benjamin Harrison was born here, at the home of his grand-
father, William Henry Harrison, in North Bend, Ohio. (The
President Benjamin Harrison Home, Indianapolis, Indiana.)

and worked in a house built for him by his father, and there
he brought a wife in 1824. They had three children before
her death in 1830. One of the children died at about the same
time.

A year later, John Scott Harrison married again. His
second wife was Elizabeth Ramsey Irwin, of Mercersburg,
Pennsylvania. Elizabeth Irwin was of Scottish descent and
was the daughter of a U.S. Army captain. Her sister, Jane,
had married John Scott's older brother, William. Elizabeth
met John when she was visiting her sister and brother-in-law
in Ohio.

It was a happy and devoted marriage. John Scott and Elizabeth shared a strong religious faith and were dutiful members of the Presbyterian Church. Elizabeth not only mothered John Scott's two surviving small children by his first wife but gave him 10 more children, seven boys and three girls. Benjamin was the second of the 10, born on August 20, 1833, in his grandfather's home at North Bend. He was christened with the honored family name that had belonged to the Signer and to four generations of Harrisons before him. He also was named after an uncle, Dr. Benjamin Harrison, one of John Scott's younger brothers.

Although the early 19th century was a time of large families, it was also a time of disease, hardship, primitive medical treatment, and frequent family sorrows. Three of John Scott's and Elizabeth's boys and one of the girls died when they were still infants. But young Ben, as he soon came to be called, was one of the lucky ones. He was a survivor.

Frontier Boyhood

Ben's boyhood was like that of any farm boy in the new states that had been created from the Northwest Territory not many years before his birth. He helped his father and the hired men feed the livestock, plant corn, gather hay, water the vegetable garden, milk cows, and perform a hundred other tasks. Days began as soon as the sun came up and ended not long after sunset.

It was not an easy life, and it was made even more difficult for Ben's parents by the many problems they faced as the years passed. In addition to the deaths of three of their children, they had to cope with a great deal of illness in the rest of the family. Colds, influenza, scarlet fever, and lung infections seemed to plague the Harrison household year after year — although Ben was one of the healthier Harrisons.

The costs of frequent doctors' visits and of medicine led to money shortages.

John Scott Harrison had to work hard to feed his growing family and earn enough money for necessary expenses. Despite his fame, General William Henry Harrison was not an exceptionally wealthy man, and he had many children to educate and get started in life. He helped John Scott Harrison as much as he could when money was short, but in later years Ben's father often had to borrow money from other members of his family or Elizabeth's.

Ben's childhood had a lighter side, too. The Point was a wonderful place for squirrel-hunting. And the two rivers gave Ben plenty of places for swimming and fishing in the summer and duck-hunting in the fall. Fishing and duck-hunting were to remain favorite activities throughout his entire life. It was his love of outdoor life that helped Ben grow into a stocky, muscular boy, not tall but strong. He had very light blond hair—almost white in the summer, when it was bleached by hours in the sun—and clear blue eyes.

Religion had a very important role in Ben's childhood. The Harrisons attended several nearby Presbyterian churches whenever possible. Even when poor weather prevented them from going to church, they set aside Sundays as days of prayer and hymn-singing. Often they had Sunday dinner at Grandmother Harrison's home at North Bend, about four miles from the house at the Point. There the evenings were spent reading the Bible. As he grew up, Ben remained deeply committed to the Presbyterian Church and made prayer, Sunday services, and church activities part of his own life.

EDUCATION OF A PRESIDENT

In spite of his frequent money troubles, John Scott Harrison was determined to provide as good an education as possible for his children. He built a small one-room log schoolhouse on his property and managed always to have on hand a tutor for his own children and any of Ben's cousins who happened to be visiting.

The first of these teachers was Harriet Root, the niece of a Cincinnati preacher. She taught Irwin, who was a year older than Ben, Ben, and their younger brother, John. Betsy, Ben's older half-sister by his father's first marriage, later joined the class. Miss Root later said of Ben that he was "the brightest of the family, and even when five years old determined to go ahead in everything." Even at that early age, Ben demonstrated another trait that would form part of his adult character: he was, Harriet Root said, "terribly stubborn about many things."

As the children grew older, they had other tutors. One was Joseph Porter, a young man who had received a college education and who became a good friend of Ben's father. Porter, who remained at the Point for many years, predicted that Ben would be a success at one of the "yankee colleges," such as Harvard or Yale. He even suggested that Ben would do well in law.

Ben had one other source of education during his childhood. It was his grandfather's large library at North Point. As soon as Ben showed his intelligence and his love of learning, he was given permission to read from General Harrison's collection, which included many volumes on American history and the lives of famous Americans such as George Washington. The North Point library also contained books on Greek and Roman history, and Ben found these exciting.

Ben did not find novels or stories at North Point. Like many serious-minded and rather old-fashioned men of his time, William Henry Harrison had no use for fiction. But from other sources, perhaps from his tutors, Ben obtained some of the most popular novels of the day, especially the Scottish and historical romances of Sir Walter Scott. He read

William Henry Harrison, who became President in 1841 but died soon afterward, collected many history books and books about great Americans in his library at North Bend. Browsing among these volumes was part of young Ben Harrison's education. (Library of Congress.)

them over and over; his favorite was *Ivanhoe*. Although he loved to read for enjoyment as well as for instruction, Ben, like his grandfather, was a rather serious person, and he always worked hard at his studies.

Farmers' College

John Scott and Elizabeth Harrison wanted to give the best schooling they could afford to their boys. Irwin and Ben were expected to go to college, but first they needed a few years of high school, or preparatory school, as it was then called, to prepare them for college. Although tuition fees were a heavy expense, John Scott Harrison decided to send them to a preparatory school named Farmers' College. It was located in Walnut Hills, a suburb of Cincinnati. Ben arrived at Farmers' College in 1847, and the three years he spent there shaped his life in several important ways.

One of those experiences was his relationship with Dr. Robert Hamilton Bishop, a Scotsman who had had a long and distinguished career teaching history and political economics in American schools. More important, Dr. Bishop kindled in many of his students a deep and lasting love of philosophy, liberty, and public affairs. Ben was one such student. Under Bishop's direction, Ben continued the studies he had begun so enthusiastically at home. He wrote papers on subjects ranging from the exploration of North America to the difference between primitive and advanced civilizations. He developed notable skill in debates and speech-making, with Dr. Bishop always on hand to offer helpful criticism and advice.

Often in later years, Harrison said how grateful he was to have had such a good and inspiring teacher. Upon leaving Farmers' College, he wrote his thanks to Bishop: "Having for some years enjoyed the benefit of your instruction, and being now about to pass from under your care, I would be truly ungrateful were I not to return my warmest thanks for the lively interest you have ever maintained in my welfare and advancement in religious as well as scientific knowledge."

A Romantic Interest

Another important development that occurred while Ben was a student at Farmers' College was meeting a brown-eyed, brown-haired girl named Caroline Lavinia Scott. Her father, the Reverend John W. Scott, was a learned Presbyterian minister who taught chemistry and physics at the school. Ben was often invited, along with other students, to the Scott home.

Carrie, as her family and friends called her, was nearly a year older than Ben, but the two young people were immediately attracted to one another. Their acquaintanceship continued for more than a year, until 1849. At that time, the Reverend Scott moved his family to Oxford, Ohio, where he opened a school for girls.

Ben missed Carrie, but that was not the only sorrow he had to face in 1850. His mother died that year. After a period of mourning at home, however, Ben returned to the question of his future. Perhaps because of Carrie, he was not terribly disappointed when his father told him that the family did not have enough money to send him to an East Coast college, as had been planned. Instead, John Scott Harrison suggested, Ben would have to consider going to college closer to home. Ben at once decided upon Miami University—located in the small town of Oxford, Ohio.

Miami University

The college that Ben selected was proudly called "the Daughter of the Old Northwest." Another nickname sometimes given to the school was "the Yale of the Midwest," which meant that Miami compared itself to one of the oldest and best-respected colleges of the East. Miami opened in 1824, and Dr. Bishop, Ben's beloved teacher at Farmers' College, had been its first president. By the time Ben arrived there in 1850, Miami University had a total of 250 students.

Ben enrolled as a junior and soon found that college life was more regulated and more demanding than the routine of preparatory school. Each day began with religious services in the university chapel at 7:30 A.M. Mornings were devoted to classes, afternoons were study periods, and all students were supposed to be in their rooms for the night by 7:00 P.M. In spite of this strict schedule, Ben and his classmates found time for socializing and strolling around town.

Ben joined a fraternity, Phi Delta Theta, and was elected president of the Union Literary Society, a club whose members were interested in writing and debating. At this time, one of Ben's heroes was Patrick Henry, the patriotic and fiery Virginian who had spurred on the Revolution with such passionate statements as "Give me liberty or give me death." Ben, too, proved to be a gifted speech-maker, and quickly won the notice of his professors and fellow students for his skills in public speaking.

Although he was one of the hardest-working students in his class, Ben managed to make many visits to the Reverend Scott's home, which was not far from the campus. On the small front porch of the Scott residence Ben and Carrie Scott renewed their friendship, which soon turned into romance. Ben spent so many evenings on the minister's front porch that his classmates teasingly called him the "pious moonlight dude."

Carrie was a light-hearted, fun-loving young woman. Although the Reverend Scott did not approve of dancing for young people, she occasionally persuaded Ben to escort her to a dancing party. Before long, Ben's letters home were filled with glowing descriptions of Carrie's charms, and his sisters wrote back that they could hardly wait to meet her.

Ben's studies and his romance with Carrie kept him busy during his two years at Miami University, but not too busy to continue his religious growth. One of his professors was a famous Presbyterian minister, the Reverend Dr. Joseph Claybaugh. In 1850 Claybaugh held a series of "revival" meetings on the campus, at which he preached to the young men and encouraged them to devote their lives to God. Ben attended one of these meetings and was so deeply moved that he renewed his religious faith and formally joined the Presbyterian church as an adult member.

Ben's family was delighted at this development. His father and sister wrote letters encouraging him to become a minister. The Reverend Scott, Claybaugh, and some of Ben's other teachers echoed this advice. All of them were impressed by the young scholar's intelligence, seriousness, devotion to duty, and deep religious feeling. As his graduation from Miami approached, Ben himself was drawn to the ministry. He believed, and would believe all his life, that the highest of all human goals was to serve and honor God. But he also believed that people could serve God in a variety of ways, and he was determined to make up his own mind about his future.

Chapter 3
Hoosier Lawyer

By the time Ben Harrison was ready, at 18, to graduate from Miami University, two important things had happened. First, he and Carrie had become secretly engaged to be married—secretly, because most parents at that time did not want their children to make marriage plans until they could support themselves. Second, he had decided to become a lawyer.

The reasons for the second decision are not known, but it is possible that young Harrison already was thinking about politics. At that time, as today, most politicians began their careers as lawyers. If he was thinking of a political career, Ben certainly had the example of his famous grandfather to inspire him. In addition, his father was about to begin a career in politics, serving in the U.S. House of Representatives from 1853 to 1857. Whatever his reasons, Benjamin Harrison's mind was made up. He was going to be a lawyer, not a minister as his sisters and some of his professors had hoped.

June 24, 1852, was a proud day for Ben Harrison and his family. On that day, he graduated from Miami University, third in his class. His commencement speech—on the topic "The Poor of England"—was one of 16 speeches made that day. Fortunately, it came third on the program, so the audience did not have to wait long to hear Ben speak. Harrison's college days were over. Now it was time to make his way in the world.

BECOMING A LAWYER

Before starting to study law, Ben first spent the summer following his graduation resting and restoring his energy at the Point. Five years of studying for long hours had tired him and weakened his health. He hiked around the farm, fished and hunted, and helped with the chores. Evenings were spent in quiet conversation with his father, who helped him plan his legal studies.

Until that time, the usual way of becoming a lawyer was through a kind of on-the-job training. Young men worked in the offices of established attorneys, serving as clerks (somewhat like secretaries), assistants, librarians, and whatever else was needed. In this way, they gained practical knowledge about the legal profession and also made themselves known to the judges and other attorneys who made up the local judicial system. At the same time, the law clerks followed courses of reading and study laid out for them by the attorneys they served. When the clerks were determined to be ready to practice on their own, they took the state bar examination. Upon passing this examination, they were permitted to practice law.

This system of study had worked well for many generations. Thomas Jefferson and Andrew Jackson were just two of the many great American leaders who had studied law as clerks. Recently, however, several colleges had opened law schools, and the classroom method of study was beginning to rival that of clerkship. One such college was located in Cincinnati, and for a while Harrison and his father considered its merits. Finally, though, they decided in favor of the old, reliable clerkship method. Ben's father had a good friend named Bellamy Storer who was a partner in a Cincinnati law firm, and he advised his son to apply to Storer for a clerkship position.

Storer and Gwynne

Harrison arrived in Cincinnati in the fall of 1852. Just 19 years old, the hustle and bustle of the fast-growing city must have been both exciting and a little scary to the young man. The Queen City, as Cincinnati was called, was in the middle of a tremendous boom. Settlers from Pennsylvania and other eastern states, as well as large numbers of immigrants from Germany and Ireland, were flocking to the city and its suburbs. They worked in its many new factories or in the docks and warehouses that handled the growing Ohio River trade.

Things went well for Harrison upon his arrival in Cincinnati. He had a ready-made new home with a married older sister whose husband was a doctor in the city. Furthermore, he found himself welcomed in the law office of Storer and Gwynne. His father's old friend, Bellamy Storer, guided Harrison's reading and willingly shared his knowledge and experience with the ambitious young clerk. Harrison was to work in Storer's office for more than a year.

Early Marriage

Although he threw himself eagerly into his law studies and his clerking duties, Harrison was not in a happy frame of mind. Before long, he decided that he hated city life, with its grime and noise. He missed the fresh air and outdoor pleasures of the Point. In addition, he began to repeat the pattern of overwork and exhaustion that had weakened his health during his college years. He worked and studied constantly and seemed to his best friend, John Anderson, to have no amusements. His one luxury was an occasional cigar. Both Ben and his brother Irwin had started smoking cigars at a young age, in spite of their parents' protests.

Most unsatisfying to Harrison at this time was his separation from Carrie. She was finishing her own studies at her father's school in Oxford, where she was also teaching music and sewing to the younger girls. While at Miami University, Ben had grown used to seeing Carrie almost every day, and now he missed her dreadfully. He visited the post office daily, hoping to receive a letter from her. On the days when he didn't get one he moped. He even complained to Anderson that the postal clerks were teasing him for showing up so frequently. Soon Harrison was thinking about getting married even before his clerkship was completed.

Money, of course, was the chief obstacle to an early marriage. As Anderson reminded Harrison in a letter, "Coffee and muffins for two are not paid for by affection." Ben could barely afford to keep himself in Cincinnati. How would he and Carrie live if they got married?

Finally, during the summer of 1853, Harrison decided that he would complete the last six months of his law training at the Point, reading and studying under Storer's direction. This meant that he and Carrie could live on the family farm. They would be able to help take care of things at home once John Scott Harrison left for his congressional seat in Washington. After much discussion, Harrison managed to convince both his father and Carrie's that this plan was reasonable. To his delight, both parents gave their consent to the marriage. It was decided that the wedding would take place in October.

Harrison's final weeks in Cincinnati were the happiest he spent there. The law office of Storer and Gwynne was burdened with paperwork that kept him busy until late at night, yet he daydreamed of the day soon to come when he would return to the Point with his bride.

The most unpleasant part of the wedding preparations, Ben discovered, was shopping for a proper groom's outfit.

Harrison married Caroline Scott, his high school sweetheart, in 1853. This photograph of her was taken many years later, in 1889, when she was First Lady of the White House. (Library of Congress.)

He hated shopping and fussing with his clothes at any time, and he took a dislike to the clothing that was standard for bridegrooms at that time: a gray suit with a white vest.

Tiring of the endless discussions with his friends and his brother Irwin about vests, coats, and the rest, Harrison took a bold step and bought an ordinary all-black suit with a black satin vest. That was regarded as rather daring and unusual for a wedding. But Harrison was not trying to make a fashion statement; he was simply being practical. He thought he would be more comfortable in a new black suit—and he could always use it in court after he became a lawyer.

The incident of the wedding suit shows the essence of Harrison's character: he was stubborn, practical, and always inclined to do what felt right to him rather than to listen to the opinions of others. These characteristics would both help and hurt him in the future, when he became President of the United States.

At last the great day arrived. On the morning of Wednesday, October 19, 1853, Ben and Carrie were married in Dr. Scott's house in Oxford. The bride's father performed the ceremony. Harrison wore the black suit, and Carrie dressed modestly in a gray traveling suit. She had agreed with Harrison that a large, expensive wedding was out of the question in view of their uncertain financial circumstances. Family members and a few close friends were the only guests, and the ceremony was followed by a simple wedding breakfast. Afterward, the bride and groom set off for the Point.

Passing the Bar

The next six months were a delightful time, just as Harrison had hoped. While he and Carrie managed the farm at the Point, Ben continued his reading and studying of law, making occasional short trips to Cincinnati for courtroom appearances and meetings with Bellamy Storer. There was also time for fishing, hunting, and writing letters to Anderson and other friends. In these letters, Harrison reported that married life was "an infinitude of quiet happiness" and that fresh air and exercise had fully restored his health. He no longer felt tired, nervous, or worried.

In early 1854, Harrison passed the Ohio bar examination. He was now a fully qualified attorney. The next step was to establish his own practice. His friends and family urged him to settle in Cincinnati, where he already was well known and where he would be close to home. But Ben decided otherwise. Showing his independence and his desire to stand on his own rather than on his family's reputation, he said, "I long to cut my leading strings and acquire an identity of my own."

As much as he disliked city life, however, Ben knew that he would have to live in a large city in order to attract enough business to survive. Therefore, he began considering some of the other cities in the Midwest. For a time, he planned to move to Chicago. But in March of 1854 he visited Indianapolis, the capital of the neighboring state of Indiana. That visit helped Ben make up his mind about where to practice law.

A HOOSIER HOME

Harrison found Indianapolis to be a pleasant city of 16,000 people, growing rapidly but not as large or as bustling as Cincinnati or Chicago. Although connected to the rest of the country by a network of new railroads, Indianapolis was still a frontier city in some ways. Delaware and Miami Indians lived on the outskirts of town, and there was excellent deer and duck hunting in the surrounding woods and swamps. Harrison also liked the location of Indianapolis. It was close enough to the Point and to Oxford to maintain strong family connections, but it was far enough away so that the young couple would have privacy and independence.

In addition to all of these features, Indianapolis was a state capital — a good place for anyone who might develop political interests or ambitions. And, although Ben wanted to stand on his own feet, he was well aware that many older Hoosiers, as the people of Indiana were called, had been his grandfather's friends when William Henry Harrison served as territorial governor from 1801 to 1809. Moreover, the famous Battle of Tippecanoe that earned William Henry his nickname took place in Indiana in 1811. Thus, Harrison was an honored name in that state. On the whole, it seems that Ben wanted to be independent of his family's name and fame — but not *too* independent.

Indianapolis appeared even more attractive when Harrison renewed his acquaintance with a cousin named William Sheets. Sheets was a somewhat older man who was a successful and popular builder and paper manufacturer in Indianapolis. He invited Ben and Carrie to stay in his house until they found a place of their own. He also assured Harrison that the city offered plenty of opportunities to a bright young lawyer and had a vigorous Presbyterian church.

Getting Started

In spite of Ben's high hopes and his determination, things did not go as well as he had expected. The newlyweds could not stay with Cousin Sheets forever, and the expense of renting quarters of their own proved high — especially when Carrie became pregnant and was unable to do housework without the help of a hired maid. To save money, Carrie returned to Oxford to live with her parents until the child was born.

Harrison found that he had to compete with a great many other eager lawyers in Indianapolis to attract clients, and he was less busy than he wanted to be. But Ben's luck took a turn for the better when two friends not only helped him obtain office space in the State Bank Building, but also got him a job in court at a salary of $2.50 a day. This gave Harrison an excellent opportunity to meet and make a good impression on other lawyers.

Before long, Ben was being asked to help prepare cases for other, more established lawyers. His great skill in making courtroom speeches and in cross-examining witnesses brought him recognition and some favorable mentions in local newspapers. Soon the governor of Indiana entrusted Harrison with an investigation on behalf of the state, and other important cases followed. Then, in 1855, came a still better piece of good fortune. A successful attorney named William Wallace invited Harrison to enter into partnership with him.

Wallace needed a partner to handle some of his cases because he wanted time to campaign for public office. On his side, Harrison needed cases in order to build up a decent income. The partnership seemed like the ideal solution to both men's needs, and they quickly became great friends. Harrison not only took care of many of Wallace's former clients but soon demonstrated his ability to attract new clients. By the end of the first year of their partnership, Wallace and Harrison were bringing in a respectable $150 a month.

FAMILY LIFE

At last, Harrison began to earn a modest but comfortable salary. This was especially welcome because he now had a son, as well as a wife, to support. Russell Benjamin Harrison was born on August 12, 1854, in Oxford, Ohio. He spent the first few months of his life with his mother at the Point because both Ben and Carrie agreed that the country was healthier for an infant than the shabby quarters that were the best Harrison could afford in Indianapolis.

Soon after teaming up with Wallace, however, Ben was able to move his family into a small rented house. He was overjoyed to have his wife and son with him and to feel that the worst of his financial troubles were behind him. His happiness was further increased when a daughter was born on April 3, 1858. He and Carrie named the baby Mary Scott Harrison, but she was known by the nickname "Mamie." As soon as he could afford it, Ben moved his growing family to a larger and more comfortable home.

Church played a central role in the Harrisons' social life in Indianapolis. They joined the First Presbyterian Church, which had been recommended by Cousin William Sheets. Both Ben and Carrie quickly took on responsibilities of leadership in the church. Ben was made a deacon, or church officer, in 1857, and only four years later he was elected an elder, or senior official, of the church. He taught Sunday school classes and was a leader of young men's groups, such as the Young Men's Christian Association (YMCA). Carrie contributed needlework to church fairs and helped organize social events, such as suppers and picnics, for church members.

Once Ben's career was on a solid footing, he and Carrie found themselves well pleased with the city that they had chosen to call home. They liked their church and the new friends that they made, and Ben found the lively legal and political atmosphere of the state capital very much to his taste. When he received an invitation from the citizens of the small town of Shelbyville, Indiana, to move his practice to that community, he was honored by their confidence in him—but he felt no hesitation in turning down the offer. Indianapolis was his home now, and he planned to stay there.

Chapter 4
Republican Politics

W ork, family, and church were not Benjamin Harrison's only concerns during the second half of the 1850s. Once he had established his law practice and home in Indianapolis, he found himself drawn into another area of activity: politics.

It was only natural, of course, that the grandson of a U.S. President and the son of a congressman should get involved in political affairs. Harrison had been interested in history since his childhood, and an interest in the political events of the past generally leads to an interest in current political events. Both his teachers and his father had encouraged Ben to study and think about the principles on which the United States government was based.

Throughout his early life, Harrison had many opportunities to hear his father discuss with friends the political issues and news of the day. Later, John Scott Harrison's letters to his son from Washington were filled with accounts of debates in the House of Representatives and with the older man's descriptions of his fellow politicians.

Congressman Harrison's views on political subjects were, in general, rather negative. He found that the actual day-to-day practice of politics was sometimes less honorable and less attractive than the ideas and theories that lay behind it. He formed unflattering opinions of many prominent Washingtonians, and he repeatedly cautioned his son not to get involved in politics and government because so many politicians were "knaves"—that is, men without honor or morals.

Although Ben respected his father's views, he held quite different opinions. He was ready to admit that many men in public life were, as his father said, knaves. But he also felt that the only way to improve matters was for upright, honest men to enter the political arena—men like himself. He began to take an active part in local party politics.

THE BIRTH OF A POLITICAL PARTY

Harrison got involved in political life at an especially exciting and dramatic point in American political history. The year of his move to Indianapolis was the same year that a very rare event occurred: a new political party was born. The party that arose in 1854 was to have an enormous influence on the rest of Harrison's life. To understand what lay behind the formation of this new party, it is necessary to know something about the history of political parties in the United States.

Republicans and Federalists

The nation's founders carefully planned the major features of the American political system. They agreed that the country would be a democracy, or "government by the people," in which public officials would be elected by vote. They designed a three-part structure of government, consisting of the executive branch (the President), the legislative branch (Congress), and the judicial branch (the Supreme Court). They intended that each branch of government should have some control over the others so that no single branch could become too powerful. But one feature of the American government that was *not* planned by the Founding Fathers was a system of competing political parties.

Although political parties arose almost as soon as the first President took office, the Constitution does not call for them. Some of the Founding Fathers even expressed the hope that America would remain free of the party divisions that were found in English political life.

Nevertheless, in a nation that takes pride in its citizens' freedom to think and speak as they please, it is natural that people who share the same opinions should group themselves together. That is how the first political parties were born during the presidency of George Washington. The first President himself did not belong to any particular party, but the members of his Cabinet and of the first Congress gradually clustered into two groups. These two groups were divided over the question of power in the new republic—in particular, the power of the federal government itself.

Although the Constitution outlined the broad structure of government, it left many areas open to the interpretation of the nation's leaders. Some of these leaders favored a strong central, or federal, government that would have considerable control over the individual states and would have any powers that were not specifically ruled out by the Constitution. Others favored states' rights—that is, they wanted the federal government to have only those powers specifically granted to it by the Constitution, and they wanted the states to have considerable individual freedom.

The first group, those who felt that the balance of power should lie with the federal government, were called the Federalists. John Adams and Alexander Hamilton were their early leaders. The second group, the states' rights people, came to be called the Democratic-Republicans, or simply the Republicans. Thomas Jefferson was their spokesman and the first of that group to become President.

Thus, before the administration of the first President had ended, two opposing political parties had formed in the United

States. The two-party system has operated for most of the years since that time, although there have been short periods when there was only one strong party and other periods when a third party gained some significant power.

Democrats and Whigs

Although the two-party system got an early start in the country's history, it faltered after a dozen years or so. The Federalist Party lost strength after President John Adams left office in 1801, and a decade later it had all but disappeared. For several decades, the Democratic-Republican Party was the only political party in the country, but that party did not remain unified. Rival groups formed around differences of opinion, and these groups competed with each other for power. During the 1820s, the Democratic-Republican Party split into two opposing parties.

One of these parties was led by Andrew Jackson, who became President in 1829. He and his followers called themselves Democrats. They considered themselves to be a continuation of the old Republican Party of Washington's and Jefferson's day. Today, historians consider Jackson's Democrats to be the origin of the modern Democratic Party.

The other party that was formed when the Democratic-Republican Party split first adopted the name National Republican Party. Before long, however, the National Republicans changed their name to Whigs. After about 1830, the Whig Party flourished in opposition to the Democratic Party. For several decades, political life in America was a contest between Whigs and Democrats. The two-party system had been established once again, and this time it was here to stay.

Among the great Whig leaders during the middle of the 19th century were Senators Henry Clay of Kentucky and Daniel Webster of Massachusetts. Ben's grandfather, William

Henry Harrison, was one of two Whig candidates to be elected President (the other was Zachary Taylor). Ben's father, John Scott Harrison, was a loyal Whig, and Ben was expected to be one, too. But in the matter of party loyalty, just as in the matter of his career and his marriage, he proved to have a mind of his own.

The Kansas-Nebraska Act

Harrison came of age as a voter when the Whig Party—the party of his grandfather and father—was falling apart. The party's troubles were rooted in the same issue that threatened to tear the country apart during the 1850s: slavery.

As far back as the American Revolution, slavery had posed a problem. The slaveholders of South Carolina and other southern colonies had insisted that independence from England must not threaten their right to own slaves. Jefferson was just one of many colonial leaders who were tormented by doubts and fears arising from slavery. He and many others knew that slavery was wrong. However, they did not know how to end it because they did not believe that black and white people could live together in liberty as equals. For decades after the founding of the United States, people who were troubled by the existence of slavery clung to the hope that it would eventually die out if it were not allowed to spread.

One person who held this belief was President James Monroe, who in 1820 was responsible for an act called the Missouri Compromise. Under the Missouri Compromise, the Mississippi River Valley that had been acquired from France in the Louisiana Purchase was divided into a northern and southern part. The southern part of the Louisiana Territory was to be made into slave states. But the northern part of the Territory was to enter the Union only as free states; slavery was forbidden there.

For a few years, the Missouri Compromise managed to bring an uneasy truce. A generation later, however, it was overthrown. In 1854, Congress passed a law called the Kansas-Nebraska Act, which said that the question of slavery in the new states that were being created out of the western territories should be settled by a vote of the settlers themselves — no matter that slavery had been banned in these territories by law for more than 20 years. The Kansas-Nebraska Act horrified the powerful and well-organized antislavery movement in the North as much as it pleased the proslavery South. Both sides immediately sent hordes of settlers swarming into the territories, hoping to sway the vote. And believers on both sides engaged in riots, terrorism, even murder.

The Republicans

The wave of violence and bloodshed that swept through the West was only one result of the Kansas-Nebraska Act. Another result was the death of the Whig Party, which fell apart because its members could not agree on a position toward the act and toward slavery in general. Some Whigs had been urging their party leaders to take a stronger antislavery position. With the passage of the Kansas-Nebraska Act, these abolitionists — who got their name because they called for the abolition, or end, of slavery — felt that the time had come to separate themselves from a weak and indecisive party.

After small meetings in Wisconsin and other states, the "anti-Kansas-and-Nebraska men," as they were called at first, decided to organize themselves as a national political party. They held their first big rally in Jackson, Michigan, in July of 1854. Former Whigs were not the only ones in attendance; many Democrats who favored a strong antislavery stand also joined the new party. There in Jackson, the party members chose a name: Republicans. They stood for a strong federal government, limited states' rights, and an immediate end to slavery.

The Know-Nothings

The American Party, to which John Scott and Irwin Harrison pledged their allegiance in the 1850s, did not outlive the decade. It got its start during the 1840s, in a movement that was based on fear of immigrants, especially Roman-Catholic immigrants from Ireland and Italy. Many uninformed Americans believed that these newcomers were anti-Americans who would be more loyal to their church than to the American government. In addition, some laborers felt that newcomers to America's shores were taking jobs away from "real" Americans. Strong feelings against foreigners, and even violence against them, became common in cities such as Boston, New York, and Philadelphia, which had large populations of immigrants.

A number of secret societies were formed to promote the unity of "true Americans" against foreigners and Catholics. Some of them had patriotic-sounding names, like the Order of the Star Spangled Banner. Out of these widespread groups grew the Know-Nothing movement, a cluster of secret societies whose members identified themselves with passwords, secret handshakes, and other rituals. If questioned about the society by outsiders, the members were supposed to say, "I know nothing." This practice gave rise to the nickname "Know-Nothings."

The Know-Nothing movement quickly gained political strength and officially became the American Party in 1854. Although it was not very flattering to their intelligence, members of the party continued to use the name Know-Nothings for several years. In the mid-1850s, Know-Nothing candidates were elected to governorships or important legislative posts in seven states. But after the defeat of their presidential candidate, Millard Fillmore, in 1856, the Know-Nothings lost ground. Many northern Know-Nothings had antislavery leanings, and they went over to the Republicans.

The remnants of the American Party reorganized in 1860 under the name Constitutional Union Party and ran John Bell of Tennessee for President, but they made a poor showing. The nickname "Know-Nothing" was scornfully changed to "Do-Nothing," and the American Party died away during the Civil War. Unfortunately, the ignorance and prejudice that were the basis of the early anti-immigrant movement survived the war. They reappeared later in the form of the Ku Klux Klan and other racist secret societies.

The birth of the Republican Party meant the death of the Whig Party. Now that they lacked a strong organization of their own, many Whigs, including Harrison's father and his brother Irwin, joined a short-lived party called the American Party, which had sprung up in the early 1850s. The remaining Whigs split into a number of small, weak subgroups, but they could not muster much support for their candidates. The Republicans, on the other hand, held their first national convention in Philadelphia in 1856. Four years later, in 1860, their candidate, Abraham Lincoln, was elected President. By then, the Whig Party had almost completely ceased to exist.

HARRISON THE REPUBLICAN

From the start, Ben Harrison was attracted to the new Republican Party. But his growing involvement with Republicanism brought about a crisis in the Harrison clan and put a severe strain on the relationship between Ben and his father.

The younger Harrison disapproved of the Kansas-Nebraska Act because he felt that Congress had no right to overturn its earlier pledge to keep the northern part of the Louisiana Territory free of slavery. John Scott Harrison agreed with his son in this matter, and was among the members of Congress who tried their best to block the passage of the Kansas-Nebraska Act. But Benjamin Harrison went even further. He enthusiastically adopted the vigorous antislavery position of the northern abolitionists who made up the core of the new party. Here he differed sharply from his father's views.

John Scott Harrison felt that the abolitionists were too extreme and violent, and that their insistence upon ending slavery would bring about a break between the North and the South. He favored the idea of compromise and negotiation, of trying to work out a position in the middle that would be acceptable to both sides. He found himself supporting the American Party, which did not take a firm stand on the issue of slavery. Like many former Whigs, John Scott Harrison hoped that the slavery question that was tearing the country apart during the 1850s could be settled peacefully. He did not know it, of course, but by 1854 it was probably too late for a peaceful settlement.

Campaigning for the Pathfinder

Benjamin Harrison showed his enthusiasm for the Republicans as early as 1854. But it was not until 1856—the year the Republicans held their first national meeting in Philadelphia—that he was sufficiently established in his work and his home life to devote any time to political activity. His friend and partner, Will Wallace, encouraged Ben to help campaign for the Republican presidential candidate, John C. Frémont. Known as the Western Pathfinder because of his earlier successes as an explorer in the American West, Frémont took an antislavery position. In a three-cornered election race, he was opposed by James Buchanan, the Democratic candidate, and Millard Fillmore, the American Party candidate.

As the presidential campaign raged during the summer of 1856, so did a war of words between Ben and his father. Early in the summer, John Scott Harrison wrote to his son gloating that the Republicans had been defeated in some local elections in Indiana. He said, "I see by the papers that your Republican ticket was badly beaten. If you want to be successful, you must run up the true blue American flag." The elder Harrison campaigned on behalf of Fillmore and actually helped support a movement to turn voters against Frémont because he was a Catholic—an unheard-of thing for a President at that time. Many friends of the Harrison family thought that his father's example and advice would cause Benjamin to give up his Republicanism and join the American Party. But they reckoned without his stubborn independence.

The younger Harrison stuck to his Republican position. His relationship with his father grew so bad that the elder Harrison refused to visit Benjamin and his family in Indianapolis. On election day, both the Republicans and the Americans were disappointed. With the former Whig vote split between the two new parties, neither candidate could win enough votes to claim victory. James Buchanan, the Democratic candidate, was elected President.

First Political Posts

John Scott Harrison hoped that Frémont's defeat would bring about the downfall of the Republican Party. At the very least, he thought, his son might abandon the party. But although he was a wise and shrewd politician in some ways, the elder Harrison was quite wrong on this occasion. Not only did the Republican Party survive Frémont's loss, but it gained strength after 1856. It was the American Party that dwindled and died. And not only did Benjamin Harrison remain a Republican, but he ran for public office on the Republican ticket.

In May of 1857, Harrison was elected city attorney of Indianapolis, at a salary of $400 a year. It was not a highly regarded position, but it gave the 23-year-old Harrison a chance to identify himself with the local Republican Party organization and to prove his abilities and his party loyalty. His father and his brother Irwin remained greatly disappointed that Benjamin did not see eye to eye with them on political questions. Irwin, now an Army officer serving in the Kansas Territory, was particularly angry when Benjamin tried by letter to convert him to Republicanism. He wrote back that he scorned the Republicans and that he wished his brother would join the American Party. Then he added, "But enough of politics," and went on to write of family matters in a more cheerful tone.

In truth, the Harrison family was too affectionate to remain divided for long over a question of politics. As important as they believed the issues of slavery and of political parties to be, John Scott Harrison and his sons respected each other's rights to their own opinions. By 1858, when Benjamin was appointed state secretary of the Indiana Republican Committee, John Scott Harrison had made peace with his son.

Ben's father was home from Congress now, and letters and visits from Benjamin and his family were one of his biggest delights. He did not want party politics to keep them apart. In spite of his distaste for the Republicans, he was proud of his son and had faith in his judgment and honor. He also believed that the younger Harrison could make a very successful career in politics. He wrote to Benjamin in January of 1858, "I look forward to a period in the future when you may occupy a high position among the political men of Indiana."

Even as a proud father, John Scott Harrison did not foresee that his son would one day occupy the highest position in the land. Although he would not live to see his son become President, John Scott Harrison is the only man in United States history who was the son of one President and the father of another.

Chapter 5

The Civil War

As the 1850s drew to a close, Benjamin Harrison had good reason to be happy. He had chosen a path for himself—and the choice had been a good one. He was successfully established as a lawyer, a respected citizen, and a church member in Indianapolis. He had married his childhood sweetheart and had two healthy children. His first ventures into politics were also successful. He had won his first political contest and become city attorney, and the Republican Party had chosen him as its state secretary. Best of all, the coldness that had grown up between Benjamin and his father had been overcome by the warmth of their sincere affection.

In short, everything was going well for Benjamin Harrison as 1860 approached. He might have expected the next few years to pass just as smoothly. But momentous events were to occur that would disrupt the lives not just of the Harrisons of Indianapolis, but of all the people of the United States.

The conflict that had been brewing between the North and the South, between the abolitionists and the slaveholders, broke out in the Kansas Territory and elsewhere. It was not simply the question of slavery that was at issue. The underlying issue was: Could individual states or sections of the country do as they pleased? Or did the federal government have the right and the power to overrule the states?

The core of the conflict between North and South was the very definition of the Union that held the states together. By 1860, some of the southern states were testing the limits of that union, claiming that they would withdraw, or secede, from the United States rather than submit to a federal government dominated by abolitionists.

RISING REPUBLICANISM

In the meantime, Indianapolis found itself deeply divided over the issue of slavery and the other questions that also divided the rest of the country and its political parties. Hoosiers took part in fierce debates, in which members of each political party insulted their opponents about half of the time and tried to convert them the rest of the time.

But Ben Harrison had no doubts. He had cast his lot with the Republican Party because he shared its basic beliefs, and he remained loyal to the party. By January of 1860, he had decided to run as a Republican for a new public office – reporter of the State Supreme Court of Indiana.

This position not only carried a great deal of prestige and honor, it was also very profitable. The reporter had the duty of keeping accurate records of all cases that came before the Indiana Supreme Court. He then published reports of these cases in one or more volumes each year, and he kept the profits earned from the sale of these *Indiana Reports*. Because almost every lawyer or law office in the state found it necessary to buy all of the volumes, the reporter was able to make a handsome income from these sales. This was the sought-after post that Harrison wanted. He announced his candidacy shortly after the first of the year.

About a month later, in February, the Republicans held their state convention in Indianapolis. Convention delegates agreed on a candidate for governor without much trouble, but the nomination for supreme court reporter was a battle. Three candidates sought the nomination, and their merits were hotly argued on the convention floor. Finally, drawing upon his speech-making gifts, Harrison delivered a rousing talk to the delegates that won him the nomination. Only 26 years old, he had just won his first major political fight. For the rest of his life, Harrison loved to reminisce about the state convention of 1860 and how he won the nomination.

Canvassing and Stumping

During the months before the election, Harrison was kept busy with work at his law office and with party activities that were directed by Republican headquarters. The most important of these activities were canvassing and stumping. Canvassing consisted of meeting people face to face and asking for money contributions to the campaign or for their votes. Stumping, or speech-making, got its name from the old frontier practice of addressing crowds or political rallies from atop anything that happened to be handy, such as a tree stump. Of the two activities, Harrison much preferred stumping. He was a good orator, and he enjoyed using his gifts of logic, clear presentation, and a vigorous tone of voice to electrify a crowd.

On the other hand, Harrison had a lifelong tendency to be a bit quiet and withdrawn when he was dealing with people individually. Some recognized this quietness as being caused by nervousness or shyness. Others, however, misinterpreted it as snobbishness. As a result, Harrison acquired something of a reputation as being stuck up and proud. This undeserved reputation remained with Harrison throughout his career. It caused many people, especially members of the lower economic classes, to turn against him.

Harrison's strength as a campaigner lay in stumping. This was never more clearly shown than in the first campaign speech he ever gave. It took place in the early spring of 1860, in the small but growing town of Lebanon, about 25 miles north of Indianapolis. Harrison was scheduled to address the crowd just after a speech by a popular former Whig named Caleb Blood Smith. Smith gave a lively and colorful speech, full of comical insults to the Democrats that made the crowd roar with appreciative laughter.

After Smith finished his speech, someone began to introduce Harrison. Few people in Lebanon had ever heard of Benjamin Harrison. The audience took a look at the short, quiet, 26-year-old standing with his hands in his pockets on the stage and began to drift away. It did not seem likely that this young fellow could have anything interesting or exciting to say.

Here was a critical and embarrassing moment. In another few minutes the crowd would be entirely gone, and Harrison would be left to make his speech to an empty field. He took action. Abruptly, he stepped forward and began to speak, and, as a newspaper reporter described the scene years later:

> Mr. Harrison had the same sharp, rasping voice that became famous in after years, and with almost his first utterance he caused the crowd to pause. Some stopped a moment to look at the boyish figure as he stood on the stand, with his hands in his trouser pockets.
>
> Another sentence shot out, reaching to the very edge of the crowd, and more of them paused to listen. They began to get back toward the stand, drop into their seats, or lean against some of the trees. Those who had got some distance away looked back and saw the deserted seats being filled up, and they, too, came back.

This small victory was the first of many triumphs that Harrison was to experience over a lifetime of public speaking. He always had the ability to present his arguments clearly and sharply, and to attract his listeners in spite of themselves. The Republican Party put that ability to good use in 1860 by sending Harrison stumping through the cities and towns of Indiana. The young lawyer was campaigning for himself, of course, but he was also compaigning on behalf of the Republican Party's candidate for President—a tall, gangly former Hoosier named Abraham Lincoln.

The Elections of 1860

The campaign of 1860 was a lively one. Perhaps the people were stirred by secret fears that the nation was heading toward war. Whatever the reason, they turned out by the thousands for torchlight parades, rallies, and marches in honor of the candidates. In a strange hint of the war that was just around the corner, some of the parades were led by drum and bugle corps and had a distinctly military air.

Indiana's state election was held in October. The results brought joy to the Harrison household—Benjamin Harrison was elected State Supreme Court reporter by a majority of 9,688 votes. There was rejoicing at the Point as well, and even John Scott Harrison sent a special message of congratulations to his son. But he added that he hoped Lincoln would not be elected President.

When November came and the national presidential election was held, John Scott Harrison was disappointed as Republicans across the country cheered. Lincoln—who had firmly and repeatedly stated that he would use whatever means were necessary to keep all of the states in the Union—had been elected President. He would take office the following March. The stage was set for the greatest conflict in the nation's history.

THE CALL TO ARMS

Tension grew during the final days of 1860 and the beginning of 1861. In December 1860, South Carolina seceded from the Union and declared itself independent of the United States. Six other southern states followed in February 1861. President Buchanan was glad to be leaving office before the storm broke, and he took no action. The nation waited uneasily. What would Lincoln do? Would he compel the southern states to return? Would there be war?

Meanwhile, Lincoln was slowly making his way from Springfield, Illinois, to Washington to be inaugurated. At each of a number of stops along the way, Lincoln made a brief speech to the citizens, reminding them that they stood at a crossroads in their nation's history. One such stop was in Indianapolis. Harrison was in the crowd outside a downtown hotel called the Bates House when the President-elect asked his audience: "Shall the Union and shall the Liberties of this country be preserved to the latest generations?" Harrison noted at the time that "it seemed hardly to be a glad crowd, and he not to be a glad man." There was little feeling of celebration as Lincoln advanced to his presidency. Rather, the country waited in tension and suspense to see how the crisis of southern secession would be handled.

In the meantime, Harrison found himself working harder than ever. He was busy with his legal cases during the day and increasingly busy preparing his first volume of *Indiana Reports* in the evenings. He was unhappy about spending so many hours away from his family, and soon the old pattern of overwork and exhaustion began to appear. But he felt that he had to do well at both his law practice and his reporter's job, so long hours of work could not be avoided. In order to have a quiet place to work on the *Reports* without interruption, he set up a small office in the basement of his church.

It was there, in April of 1861, that Harrison received word that southern troops had fired upon the Union-held Fort Sumter in the harbor of Charleston, South Carolina. The dispute between the North and the South had finally gone beyond words. Now it was a matter for bullets. President Lincoln sent out a call for volunteers to form a Union Army. The Civil War had begun.

To Fight or Not

As soon as war broke out, Harrison faced an agonizingly difficult choice. Should he enlist in the Army or not? As a Republican who had supported Lincoln and opposed southern secession, he felt the need to back up his beliefs on the battlefield. If his own party and the government he had helped to elect were fighting to preserve the Union, then surely, he told himself, it was his duty to join the fight. In addition, there was the military tradition of his grandfather, William Henry Harrison, to live up to. Old Tippecanoe had been a professional soldier and a good one, and his grandson dreaded being accused of cowardice.

At the same time, Harrison had a wife and two small children to support. What would happen to their home and to his law practice if he enlisted? What would happen to the children if he were killed in battle? These questions troubled Harrison deeply. It was a relief to learn that the first rush of Hoosier volunteers yielded twice as many soldiers as Lincoln had asked for from Indiana. Because there seemed to be no shortage of manpower at the moment, Harrison decided that it was all right for him to stay home and continue his business and family life.

First Year of War

The first months of the war were a time of mixed sorrow and happiness for Ben and Carrie. They were deeply grieved in June of 1861 when their third child died at birth. That same month, however, they received the glad news that a regiment of Indiana volunteers had won distinction in the fighting in Virginia. Irwin Harrison, Benjamin's brother, and Henry Scott, Carrie's brother, were officers in this regiment.

Meanwhile, in Indianapolis, Harrison prospered. His law firm was busy—too busy, he sometimes felt. Will Wallace was still wrapped up in campaigns for various Republican posts in the city and county, and Harrison sometimes referred to him rather bitterly as a partner who had not done "a lick of work" in months. Finally, in December of 1861, the two men decided to end their partnership in order to preserve their friendship.

Harrison was not without a partner for long, however. Less than two weeks after the end of Wallace and Harrison, a new sign appeared on Washington Street. It read "Harrison and Fishback." Harrison's new partner was William Pinkney Fishback, usually called "Pink." He and Harrison had a thriving business from the start. This success, together with the income from the first few volumes of the *Indiana Reports,* made it possible for Harrison to buy a family home at the corner of Alabama and North Streets. It was a handsome old two-story house with a large yard and a stable.

Despite all these business and domestic activities, Harrison followed the war news every day. As 1862 approached, it began to appear that the war might be a lengthy one. Like almost everyone else in the Union, Ben had expected the fighting to last three months at most. Long before the summer was over, he had believed, Union soldiers would have quelled the Confederate rebellion and would come marching home again.

But that did not happen. To the dismay of President Lincoln and the North, the South put up a brilliant and determined fight. Moreover, the leaders of the Union Army proved to be weak just when strength was desperately needed. Time and time again the Union forces appeared to be on the verge

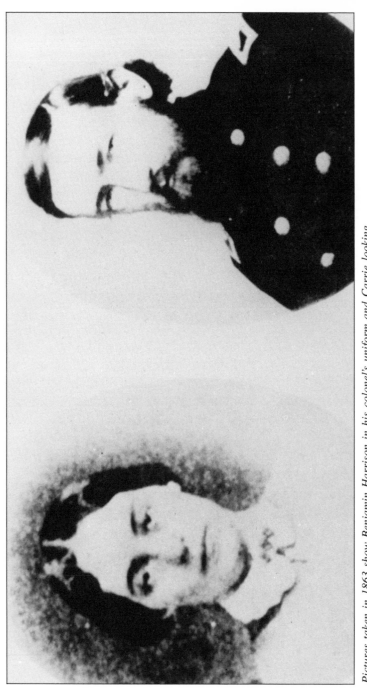

Pictures taken in 1863 show Benjamin Harrison in his colonel's uniform and Carrie looking serious and rather sad. They did not see each other for two years, but they exchanged news of home and the battlefields in frequent letters. (The President Benjamin Harrison Home, Indianapolis, Indiana.)

of a decisive victory, only to let it slip away. The war dragged on, and by the end of 1861 most people realized that it was going to be a long, bitter affair.

The 70th Indiana Regiment

In the summer of 1862, Governor Oliver Perry Morton of Indiana issued a call for more volunteer troops. This time, the response was not what he had hoped for. Only a few men enlisted. This time, too, Harrison had made up his mind to serve if he was needed. When Harrison and his former law partner, Will Wallace, visited the governor—who was also the head of the Republican Party in Indiana—Morton complained that he needed more volunteers. When Harrison volunteered on the spot, Morton instantly appointed him a second lieutenant, with the power to enlist other volunteers. Harrison turned to Wallace and promptly enlisted him as his first recruit.

During the weeks that followed, Lieutenant Harrison had to work hard to enlist enough men to complete a regiment. By August, however, he had signed up a total of 85 officers and privates, and the 70th Indiana Volunteer Regiment was officially called into existence. Harrison was promoted to the rank of colonel.

Harrison's next duty was to make the best plans he could for the welfare of Carrie and the children. He arranged that the income from the sale of the *Indiana Reports* would go to Carrie. He also persuaded Pink Fishback, who was by now a devoted friend as well as a partner, *not* to enlist. Instead, Fishback was to stay in Indianapolis and do his best to carry on the law firm for both of them.

Kentucky, Tennessee, and Georgia

The next three years made Harrison a war hero. But his part
in the war did not seem heroic at first. At times, in fact, it
was just the opposite. For a year and a half after forming his
regiment, Harrison led his men up and down muddy mountain roads in Kentucky and Tennessee, guarding Union railway lines and occasionally engaging in brief skirmishes with
small bands of Confederate soldiers. He spent a lot of time
studying textbooks and manuals of military strategy and tac-
tics. He also drilled his men until they marched and handled
their weapons with great skill, even though their fighting experience was limited.

Like many soldiers on both sides, Harrison spent months
away from his home and family. He did not receive his first
leave, with permission to go back to Indianapolis for a brief
visit with Carrie and the children, until he had been in the
field for two years. During that time, he wrote to Carrie regu-
larly, describing his life as a soldier: his joy at having a hot
meal and dry clothes after a month of rain, his fears of a surprise enemy attack in the night, his loneliness, and his pride
in the men under his command. In spite of his absence, Ben's
supporters and friends in the Republican Party saw to it that
he was re-elected State Supreme Court reporter in 1862 and
again in 1864. Temporary stand-ins were assigned to work
on the volumes that Harrison was unable to produce.

All this time, the 70th Indiana Volunteer Regiment was
moving farther south, mile by mile, as the Union Army followed its plan of carrying the war into the heart of the Confederacy. In May of 1864, many regiments and battalions of
Union troops converged on the roads that led down out of
the mountains of Tennessee into the plains of Georgia. Their
goal was Atlanta, stronghold of the Confederacy in the Deep
South. This was the famous Atlanta campaign of William
Tecumseh Sherman. Colonel Harrison led his men into the

campaign as an untested leader. After the fall of Atlanta in September, he emerged a hero –"the hero of Peachtree Creek."

WAR'S END

After the Atlanta campaign, Harrison enjoyed his first furlough, or leave, since his enlistment. He spent a joyous month at home, where he was surprised and a little saddened to see how much Russell and Mamie had grown during his absence. To his relief, Carrie was in good health and appeared to be managing the family's affairs successfully, with the income provided by Fishback's work in the law office.

In addition to a reunion with his loved ones, the visit to Indianapolis gave Harrison the chance to speak up at many meetings and rallies on behalf on President Lincoln, who was running for re-election in November. With reports of his heroism at Peachtree Creek still fresh in their minds, listeners flocked to hear Harrison.

Meanwhile, although Atlanta had fallen, the war was not yet over. All too soon Harrison's furlough came to an end, and it was time for him to rejoin Sherman's army. He and his brigade were scheduled to return to Georgia and march north with Sherman.

But late in the year, Confederate forces launched an attack on Nashville, Tennessee, in a final desperate bid for victory in the South. Harrison and his brigade were sent to Tennessee, where they camped outside the city in freezing mud and sleet. On December 15, 1864, the Confederates under General J.B. Hood attacked Nashville but were driven off. Harrison's brigade received credit for leading the advance against Hood and for a brave charge against Confederate guns. When Hood retreated southward, Harrison was ordered to follow him. But the 70th was unable to catch the fleeing Confederates, and this campaign ended in January of 1865.

Harrison was delighted to receive a second furlough,

and also to receive the promotion that Hooker had promised him. It was as a brigadier general that Harrison set off to rejoin Sherman's forces in South Carolina. When he missed Sherman there, he sailed north to Wilmington, Delaware. He arrived in Wilmington on April 12, just a few days after the surrender of the Confederate General Robert E. Lee at Appomattox, Virginia.

It was a time of wild celebration. The Confederacy had finally been defeated. The Civil War was over and the Union had been preserved. In the midst of all the excitement, Harrison was ordered south again, this time to North Carolina, where he was certain to meet up with Sherman at last. But a few days later came the tragedy of Lincoln's assassination at Ford's Theatre in Washington, D.C.

Harrison had just arrived in Raleigh, North Carolina, and was on his way to his barracks. He could not understand why the streets were empty and why the Stars and Stripes, which should have been flying triumphantly from atop each flagpole, was flying at half-mast. When he entered the barracks, he heard the shattering news: President Lincoln had been assassinated. He never forgot the grief that he felt and witnessed at that moment. Men stood and wept or cursed for hours, he later told Carrie. It was a terrible blow, following so soon on the heels of the great Union victory.

Harrison was one of the officers who was asked to deliver a eulogy, or speech of tribute, at an Army memorial service for the President. Although his words on that occasion have been lost, they may have been something like the ones he used 40 years later, when he delivered a speech about Lincoln at a banquet in Chicago. At that time, he said of Lincoln:

> Qualities of heart and mind combined to make him a man who has won the love of mankind. He is beloved. He stands like a great lighthouse to show the way of duty to all his coun-

trymen and to send afar a beam of courage to all those who beat against the winds. We do him reverence. We bless tonight the memory of Lincoln.

The Grand Review

The end of the war and the death of Lincoln did not mean that the Union soldiers could simply lay down their weapons and go home. Although he was desperately eager to resume civilian life, Harrison found that the end of a war involved a certain amount of ritual and fuss. It was decided that, in order to restore a feeling of unity and optimism to a nation that had been deeply shaken by the President's assassination, a Grand Review would be held in Washington to muster out, or dismiss, the Union troops.

The Grand Review was nothing more than a parade, but it was the biggest parade that had ever been held in the nation's capital. Regiment after regiment was to pass in review in front of an audience consisting of President Andrew Johnson, all the dignitaries of the capital, and an enormous flag-waving, cheering crowd. Harrison wrote to Carrie that it would be "the grandest military parade this country will ever see." But he added, "I would not prolong my separation from you and the children one hour to see it."

Nevertheless, Harrison was proud to ride behind Sherman at the head of his brigade, and he was prouder still to see his men receive the applause of the audience. Before they began to march, he made a speech in which he told them that the true glory of the day belonged to them: "The highest honors are due to the men who bore the cartridge and the gun. What were your officers without you?" Later in his life Harrison often spoke with pleasure of that glorious day, May 24, 1865, when he and his loyal Hoosiers marched with Sherman in the Grand Review in Washington, D.C.

Chapter 6

Private and Public Life

The Indianapolis in which Harrison found himself after the celebrations ended was a far different city from the one he had left three years before. New buildings had been built or were under construction everywhere, and the city's population had nearly doubled. Everyone expected that the end of the war would bring a boom in business and trade to the Midwest. It seemed a good time to be a popular, well-respected, established lawyer.

Harrison happily returned to his law office on the corner of Washington and Meridian Streets. He and Pink Fishback now shared the firm with a third partner, Albert Gallatin Porter. Although much of Harrison's time would be taken up with his duties as reporter for the State Supreme Court, the three men felt that they could handle a growing business. They advertised that they would specialize in cases involving the federal courts and the Indiana Supreme Court. Over the next few years, Harrison's fortunes took a definite turn for the better as his work as a lawyer and as reporter for the State Supreme Court kept him very busy.

SUCCESS IN COURT

When he was re-elected reporter of the court in 1864, Harrison hired another lawyer to collect material on the decisions that the State Supreme Court issued while he was still in the army. This assistant, John Dye, performed his task well, and Harrison was able to issue a volume of the *Indiana Reports* within a few months of his return to Indianapolis. It earned him several thousand dollars before the end of the year. But that fall Harrison was unpleasantly surprised when the federal Bureau of Internal Revenue told him that he would have to pay taxes on his income from the *Reports.* (A federal income tax had been enacted in 1862 to help finance the Civil War. Because of the many protests against the tax, Congress let it expire in 1872.) Harrison protested, claiming that his official state work was not subject to income tax. He took the matter to court. Eventually he won, and the government returned about $1,200 in taxes that he had paid under protest. To the end of his life, Harrison enjoyed telling how he had beaten the tax collectors.

In the meantime, he continued to issue new volumes of the *Reports* and to handle some of the firm's law cases. Indeed, many clients insisted that "General Harrison," the war hero and grandson of a President, handle their legal matters personally. His comfortable income allowed Harrison to make some improvements to his home, to help family members with loans, and to enroll Russell and Mamie in private schools.

Harrison also enjoyed spending a little money on himself and Carrie. On New Year's Day of 1867, she appeared wearing a new diamond pin and ring, and he wore an elegant cashmere suit. But this modest finery was the limit of Harrison's extravagance. He was always careful with money and scornful of lavish displays of wealth.

The Clem Murder Case

Harrison acted on behalf of the state of Indiana in one important case in 1868 and 1869. It concerned a gruesome double murder in the community of Cold Springs, not far from Indianapolis. Harrison was asked to help the state present its case against Nancy Clem, a townswoman who was accused of killing a local businessman and his wife for their money. Clem had been engaged in shady financial transactions — perhaps with counterfeiters. In a hard-hitting, detailed series of arguments, Harrison demolished Mrs. Clem's alibi. Then, in a remarkable eight-hour speech, he sought to convince the jury of her guilt. His skills as a persuasive, commanding, and colorful speaker were never used to better effect than in this courtroom drama. He described the discovery of the corpses and the plight of the victims' orphaned daughter:

> It was a scene to freeze one's blood . . . . Not only dead but burned! Those bleached remains, charred until scarce a vestige of her image was left! The little orphan at home waited in vain for their return that night.

Harrison's masterful speech carried the day. The jury found Mrs. Clem guilty and sentenced her to life imprisonment. And the widely reported case brought new fame to Harrison, of whom the Indianapolis *Journal* said, "No case within our knowledge was ever more skillfully conducted." Together with Harrison's family heritage and his involvement in the Republican Party, his courtroom successes led some people to predict a bright political future for him. Several years later, another and even more controversial court case would test Harrison's speech-making skills once again and make him even more famous.

The Lambdin Milligan Case

During the Civil War, northerners suspected of aiding the South were subjected to harsh penalties under President Lincoln's wartime laws. Nevertheless, secret societies sprang up in the North whose members were sympathetic with the South. One such society was the Sons of Liberty, which felt that the Union should be dissolved so that all the states could become independent. The leader of the Sons of Liberty in Indiana was a Democrat named Lambdin Milligan. In 1864, Milligan was hastily and secretly arrested and tried for treason by a military court. He was found guilty and sentenced to death, but before he was executed the sentence was changed to hard labor in prison.

In April of 1866, however, the United States Supreme Court ruled that the military court that had tried and sentenced Milligan did not have any legal right to do so. The guilty verdict was overturned and Milligan, whose health had been destroyed by his imprisonment, was released. Then, in 1868, Milligan sued the members of the military commission for $100,000 on the grounds that they had arrested and tried him illegally.

The U.S. Supreme Court had already ruled that the actions of the military commission were illegal. For this reason, the accused military men — some of whom were Harrison's friends — only wanted to reduce the amount of money they would have to pay Milligan. At the request of Republican President Ulysses S. Grant, who was sympathetic to the accused men, Harrison agreed to defend them against Milligan.

The Milligan case stirred strong feelings in Indiana and across the nation. Although Milligan's legal rights were clear, many people in the North hated to think of him winning a huge sum of money from loyal Union men. Some felt that his suffering in prison was no more than he deserved for being a Democrat who had not supported the war.

Harrison shared this view. In fact, all his life he was to be one of a group of late-19th-century politicians who were sometimes accused of "waving the bloody shirt" of the Civil War. He did not believe in letting bygones be bygones. Instead, he was fond of reminding his audiences how many Union men—fathers, husbands, and sons—had lost their lives to preserve the nation.

Harrison felt that the war was entirely the fault of the South. He also felt that southerners and northern Democrats who had not supported the war should not be allowed to escape blame. With his feelings of intense patriotism and his strict sense of right and wrong, Harrison tended to give more weight to punishment than to forgiveness.

All of this made Harrison the ideal lawyer to defend the northern commanders who had arrested Milligan. When the case came to trial in 1871, Harrison immediately seized the attention of the jury with a ringing, patriotic speech that condemned anyone who did not believe in the rightness of the Civil War. He described the flower-decked tombs of the Union dead, the wounds suffered on southern battlefields by the brave Union soldiers, and the treasonous plottings of Milligan and his fellow conspirators.

Harrison's emotional appeal worked. The jury granted Milligan's claim for damages—but reduced the amount from $100,000 to a mere five dollars! Like the Clem case, the Milligan case was a victory for Harrison, and one that carried his name to newspapers far and wide. It also won him the undying gratitude of the Republican Party, to which all of the members of the military commission had belonged.

FAMILY AFFAIRS

The years immediately following the Civil War were filled with personal as well as professional events. Much of Harrison's time and energy were taken up by family activities. When he returned from the war, he was determined to spend more time with his family than he had in the years of building up his law practice. Success was important to him, but not at the cost of spending too much time separated from his wife and children. He wrote several times to Carrie from the field that he wanted to make their family life "brighter and happier for you and the children."

For a time, Harrison was able to keep this promise. He enjoyed buggy rides with the whole family and fishing excursions with Russell. He continued to take a vigorous part in the activities of the First Presbyterian Church. As an elder of the church, he taught Sunday school for boys and young men and organized Bible study classes for the adults. He attended frequent prayer meetings and never missed a Sunday service. The church contributed to the lighter side of the Harrisons' life, too, with social occasions such as dinners and picnics. Occasionally, Ben and Carrie attended the theater or the opera together.

Over the next two years, however, the demands of Harrison's busy schedule cut into his personal life again. Between the *Indiana Reports* and the difficult court cases he was handling, not to mention Republican Party meetings and activities, he found himself working late hours. He grew tired and often complained of not feeling well. Although he had grown somewhat plump and would never look thin again, he did appear drawn and exhausted. In April of 1867, Harrison suffered a breakdown of his health that was probably brought on by sheer exhaustion. He was unable to work for several weeks.

As Carrie calmly nursed Ben back to health, he made a decision: he would give up his job as State Supreme Court reporter. It was time to put all his energy into his law practice, which he believed could support him very well. Harrison celebrated his recovery with a hunting and fishing vacation in the Minnesota lake country, and returned to Indianapolis full of enthusiasm for legal work. It was in this energetic state that he achieved some of his most brilliant courtroom triumphs of the late 1860s and early 1870s.

THE WOULD-BE GOVERNOR

Harrison may have given up his job as State Supreme Court reporter, but he most certainly did not give up his interest in politics. In 1868 he worked on the local Republican campaign for the party's presidential candidate, General Ulysses S. Grant. The campaign succeeded, and Grant was elected. When Grant ran for re-election in 1872, Harrison once again campaigned for him.

By now, Harrison again began to have political ambitions. An election was scheduled for governor of Indiana in 1872, and he wanted to be his party's candidate. He had lived in Indianapolis for 18 years, had won fame in the war, and had become a well-known attorney and church leader in the community. In addition, he was liked and respected by most Republicans throughout the state. For these reasons, he believed he had a chance to become governor.

But Harrison was not the only popular and capable Republican in Indiana. He lost his party's nomination to Thomas M. Browne. He did not give up, however. He simply waited another four years and tried again in 1876. This time he did receive the Republican nomination.

His courtroom successes helped Harrison afford this handsome new brick house on North Delaware Street in Indianapolis. The two children, Russell and Mamie, made it lively, and Carrie beautified it with carefully tended gardens. (Library of Congress.)

"Kid Gloves" and "Blue Jeans"

Harrison's Democratic opponent in the race for governor was James D. Williams. He was usually called "Blue Jeans" Williams because he wore workmen's denim trousers. The basis of Williams' campaign was that the Republicans were doing a poor job in Washington and should not be allowed to do the same in Indiana. It was true that the administration of Republican President Grant had become notorious for corruption and inefficiency. This cost the Republicans many votes in local and state elections.

Harrison's campaign relied heavily on "waving the bloody shirt." He claimed that the Democratic Party was tainted with "the leprosy of secession" and that the voters should stick with the party that had won the Civil War. In addition to campaigning on his own behalf, he threw his weight behind Rutherford B. Hayes, the Republican candidate for President.

The Indiana campaign quickly became a contest of personalities. "Blue Jeans" Williams was a lively, colorful speaker who won over his audiences with down-to-earth anecdotes and jokes. Harrison was just as good a speaker, but his tone and behavior were more dignified and formal. Some of Williams' supporters raised the old accusation of snobbery against Harrison, claiming that "the grandson," as he was called, was an upper-class politician who would serve the interests of money and business rather than those of the ordinary people.

Harrison found it impossible to relax enough to combat this unfortunate accusation. On top of this, a minor injury to one of his hands during the war meant that he often wore gloves, even when he was inside or was talking and shaking hands with people. His political enemies said that this wearing of gloves—especially expensive gloves made of kid, the skin of young goats—was a sign of social snobbery. They described Harrison as a stuck-up prig who wore gloves because he did not want to make contact with the "lower" classes. The newspapers even invented a nickname for Harrison: "Kid Gloves."

When Hoosier voters went to the polls in October of 1876, they were almost equally divided between "Kid Gloves" Harrison and "Blue Jeans" Williams. The vote was so close that both sides claimed victory. Only after several days did the Republicans admit that "Blue Jeans" had beaten Harrison by 5,000 votes.

Despite his loss, Harrison's supporters tried to encourage him by pointing out that his energetic campaign and the speeches that were reprinted in newspapers across the country had lifted him to a position of national importance. Now he was known to and admired by Republicans in all states. Although he had lost his bid for the Indiana governorship, he had emerged as a leader of the Republican Party. More important, he had prepared himself for a move into politics on the national level.

Chapter 7
Senator Harrison

As the end of the 1870s approached, Harrison found himself quite pleased with life, even though he had failed to become governor. His family life was a happy one. He had bought a fine new home on North Delaware Street, where Carrie spent many hours absorbed in her hobby, gardening. She was especially proud of her strawberry beds and grapevines, and she and the servants produced delicious jams and jellies every year.

Mamie, Harrison's daughter, was growing out of her teens. She was pretty and popular, and her life was a merry round of ice-skating parties in the winter and buggy rides in the summer. Carrie and Mamie traveled often, too, visiting family members and friends in Ohio and Pennsylvania. Russell, Harrison's son, had graduated from Lafayette College. With his father's help, he had obtained a job at the Philadelphia Mint (one of the places where the government printed and coined money).

As for Harrison himself, his life was about evenly divided between law, religion, and politics. When Pink Fishback and Albert Porter moved on to businesses of their own, Harrison brought in two other partners. He was now the senior partner in a law firm called Harrison, Hines, and Miller. At church, he continued to carry out his responsibilities as an elder, attending prayer meetings every evening. He used his speech-making skills to help raise funds to rebuild his own First Presbyterian Church and to build a new Ninth Presbyterian Church in one of the new suburbs of fast-growing Indianapolis.

"THE HARRISON HORROR"

One tragedy disturbed Harrison deeply at this time. In 1878 his father, John Scott Harrison, died. Harrison would have been saddened by the death of his beloved parent in any case, but the elder Harrison's death was followed by mysterious events that outraged the family and shocked the nation.

John Scott Harrison was buried in a family cemetery near Cincinnati. At the funeral, Benjamin noticed with dismay that the grave of a young cousin named Augustus Devin, who had died recently, appeared to have been disturbed. Immediately he thought of graverobbers, or "resurrectionists," as they were sometimes called. These were men who stole bodies from funeral homes and graveyards and sold them to medical schools.

At that time, the dissection of bodies by medical students as part of their training was a controversial practice. Surgeons pleaded that it was vitally important for doctors to study real bodies, but many people felt that the use of bodies in this way was wrong for religious reasons. So the medical schools obtained their specimens by various shady methods. They were supposed to use only the bodies of poor people or criminals who died without any families, but the supply of bodies was never big enough to meet the demand. As a result, the resurrectionists sometimes plundered graveyards, and the medical schools did not ask questions about where the bodies came from.

The Harrison family suspected that the body of their cousin had been stolen for sale to one of the local medical schools or hospitals. Within a few days, Benjamin and his brothers stormed their way into all the nearby hospitals to search for Devin's body. They did not find Devin, but at the Ohio Medical College in Cincinnati an even more terrible shock awaited them. They discovered the body of their father, John Scott Harrison, freshly robbed from its grave.

The newspapers went wild with the details of this grisly story, which they called "the Harrison Horror." Americans were appalled that the resurrectionists would rob the grave of so distinguished a citizen. Partly as a result of the public outcry, harsher laws were passed against resurrectionists. As for the Harrison family, the body of John Scott Harrison was quietly reburied, but grief and horror could not be so easily put aside. For the rest of his life, Benjamin Harrison could hardly bring himself to say the word "father," because of the strong, sorrowful feelings that the word produced.

THE ROAD TO WASHINGTON

Even after tragedy, life goes on, and Harrison's political life grew more vigorous in the late 1870s. In 1878 he made a lengthy speaking tour around Indiana to help some Republican candidates who were seeking positions in the state legislature. Meanwhile, his own political career was beginning to flourish again. Rutherford B. Hayes had been elected President in 1876, and he was grateful to Harrison for his support and help. In recognition of Harrison's loyalty to the Republican Party as well as his legal skills, Hayes appointed the Hoosier lawyer to the Mississippi River Commission in 1879.

The Mississippi River Commission

The Mississippi River, one of the world's greatest waterways, was the main route of commerce and travel in the center of the nation and in the South. Because of its frequent floods, however, it was also a dangerous waterway. The Mississippi River Commission was a seven-man board that was supposed to develop plans for improving navigation on the river and for flood control along its banks. Harrison's main goal as a commissioner was to prevent the commission from making plans that would benefit the South at the expense of the rest of the country. He did not want tax money from all over the nation being spent on dams and other engineering works that would have their greatest effect along the southern portion of the river.

Other members of the commission held opposing views. The engineers on the board quarreled with the civilians, and the northerners with the southerners. In fact, the commission accomplished nothing, because its members could not agree on anything. It was finally disbanded in 1881. Although it did not serve its real purpose, the commission reinforced Harrison's reputation as someone with connections in Washington.

The Convention of 1880

The next milestone along Harrison's road to Washington occurred at the Republican National Convention in Chicago in 1880. Harrison was selected by Hoosier Republicans to lead their delegates to the convention. At stake was the nomination for President. Hayes would not be nominated for a second term, and no one was sure who would be chosen. James Blaine of Maine was considered a likely candidate, as was John Sherman of Ohio. One prominent group of eastern Republicans even wanted to nominate Grant for a third term. There was also much speculation about the vice-presidency. Harrison's name was mentioned more than once as a possible running mate for Blaine or Sherman, but he said nothing about it and gave no clue to his feelings.

The presidential nomination was one of the most dramatic in Republican history. Ballots were cast 33 times in two days, but the result was always the same: Grant and Blaine would split the majority of delegates, with Sherman and a few other candidates each getting a sprinkling of votes. Even Harrison got one vote. But none of these men could get the 378 votes needed to make him the candidate. It looked as though the deadlock could last forever.

The 34th ballot took a different turn. When the Wisconsin delegates cast 16 votes for James A. Garfield of Ohio, there was a ripple of surprise in the smoke-filled hall. On the next ballot, Harrison made one of the shrewdest political moves of his career. Believing that neither Grant nor Blaine could win, he boldly cast Indiana's votes for Garfield. That move swung the convention in a new direction. On the next ballot, Garfield received 399 votes. Harrison was then asked to make one of the speeches that confirmed Garfield as the party's candidate for President. Everyone at the convention knew it was Harrison's support at a crucial moment that had helped nominate Garfield.

Harrison helped Garfield in other ways, too. Throughout the campaign, he stumped Indiana and other states, making speeches and leading rallies for the Republican candidate. After Garfield was elected in November, it was rumored that he planned to offer Harrison a post in his Cabinet. But the election had also brought a number of Republicans to seats in the Indiana state legislature, and these Hoosier Republicans were to have a greater influence on Harrison's future than the President.

THE SENATOR FROM INDIANA

At that time, U.S. senators were not elected by direct vote of the people. Instead, they were elected by the members of state legislatures. In January of 1881, the Indiana state legislature elected Harrison to a six-year term in the U.S. Senate. Among the many tributes and congratulations he received, one that especially moved him was a letter from a soldier in the old 70th Indiana Volunteer Regiment. "As one of your boys," it read, "being with you throughout the war, it pleases me to hear of your success." The writer concluded, "You will excuse this letter but it is from the heart."

Garfield did offer Harrison a Cabinet post, but Harrison refused it. He preferred to remain in the Senate, where he felt he could best use his legal and speech-making skills, best serve his country, and best develop his own career.

Life in Washington

Harrison arrived in Washington in time for Garfield's inauguration on March 4, 1881. Carrie and Mamie set up housekeeping in a boardinghouse on Vermont Avenue. Mamie enjoyed the social life of the capital, but she spent much time writing to Robert McKee, her sweetheart back in Indianapolis.

Russell Harrison, who was now ranching in Montana, came to the capital to visit his father, mother, and sister. While in Washington, Russell spent much of his time calling on Mary Saunders, the daughter of a Nebraska senator. Both of the Harrison children were married in 1884, during Harrison's term in the Senate. Mamie married Bob McKee, and Russell married Mary Saunders.

Harrison's first year in Washington was marred by a national tragedy. President Garfield was assassinated, and his Vice-President, Chester A. Arthur, took over the presidency. Harrison did not share the warm personal relationship with Arthur that he had enjoyed with Garfield, and his influence at the White House declined during the Arthur administration. He then campaigned for James G. Blaine of Maine, who, instead of Chester Arthur, was selected as the Republican candidate for the presidential election of 1884. But the Republi-

*Mamie, as Harrison's daughter Mary was called, was married
to Robert McKee in 1884, while Harrison was serving in the
U.S. Senate.* (Library of Congress.)

cans failed to hold on to the presidency. Grover Cleveland, a Democrat, was elected.

Senatorial Concerns

His six years in the Senate gave Harrison a valuable course in how the American political system works. He became familiar with the important issues of the day—issues with which he would later have to deal as President. He found that public service was very satisfying to his strong sense of duty.

One aspect of public life that he did not enjoy, however, was the steady stream of people who asked him for favors or government jobs. Some of these people were elderly Army veterans who had served under Harrison's grandfather and now wanted loans or pensions. Others were ambitious local politicians back in Indiana who wanted to be appointed as postmasters.

Harrison was troubled by the Republican Party's long history of giving government or civil service jobs to supporters of the party, whether they were qualified or not. In order to stop this practice—called patronage, or the spoils system— he supported a growing movement to reform the civil service. In 1883, he voted in favor of the Pendleton Act, a law that established a basis for civil service reform by requiring that some government positions must be filled by qualified candidates rather than as political favors.

On the other hand, Harrison soon became known as the "soldier's legislator" because of his support for veterans' pensions. Whenever Cleveland seemed likely to veto, or deny, a congressional request for an increase in veterans' pensions, Harrison could be counted on to oppose the veto. He also spent much time and energy trying to speed up the paperwork for the pension claims of individual Hoosier veterans who wrote to him for help. To the end of his life, Harrison believed that anyone who had fought for his country deserved the best his country could do in return.

Harrison also served on a number of congressional committees, including the Committee on Indian Affairs and the Committee on Military Affairs. His work with these two committees was not particularly noteworthy. However, as chairman of the Committee of the Territories, he managed to have a bill passed that established civil government in the Alaska Territory, which had been under military rule.

In general, Harrison strongly favored statehood for the western territories. He also believed in the importance of a strong Navy. He voted in favor of funds to buy new ships, and he supported President Arthur's moves to reorganize and modernize the U.S. Navy.

Another issue that concerned Harrison was conservation. He was one of the country's first conservationists, although he was not as committed to conservation as President Theodore Roosevelt would be a few years later. Harrison voted in favor of protecting and enlarging the national parks. He recommended that a stretch of land along the Colorado River be set aside for such protection. Although his recommendation was not followed until years later, it eventually resulted in the creation of Grand Canyon National Park.

Six busy years in Washington, broken by summers in Indianapolis and occasional holidays on the New Jersey seacoast, ended in 1887. With the election of Cleveland to the presidency in 1884, the Democrats had managed to win a majority of seats in the Indiana state legislature. When Harrison came up for re-election in February 1887, he was defeated by a Democrat named David Turpie. But the vote was close—not until the 16th ballot did Turpie win Harrison's Senate seat. Harrison was sorry to lose his place in the Senate, but he already had his next goal in mind.

Senator Harrison recommended that part of the wild, magnificent canyon of the Colorado River be preserved under federal protection. This recommendation helped create Grand Canyon National Park. (Library of Congress.)

A presidential election was scheduled for 1888, and Cleveland was certain to run for re-election on the Democratic ticket. Who would be the Republican candidate? Harrison felt that he was ready. He hoped to return to Washington in 1889 — not to the Senate, but to the White House.

Chapter 8
Centennial President

Harrison announced his intention to run for President in February of 1888, when he was making a speech in Detroit in honor of Washington's birthday. General Harrison, as he was called, rose to his feet and told the gathering, "I am a dead statesman, but I am a rejuvenated Republican." By "dead statesman," he meant that because he had lost his last bid for elected office, he could claim no great stature in Washington. But by calling himself a rejuvenated—that is, reborn or re-energized—Republican, he meant that he was more committed to his party than ever. He also meant that both he and the Republican Party were ready for a new start, or a new role. The phrase caught on, and Harrison's theme for the rest of the year was "Rejuvenated Republicanism."

Republicans from around the nation gathered in Chicago in June of 1888 to nominate a presidential candidate. James Blaine of Maine, who had come close to being President several times before, was expected to be the Republicans' choice. But years of politicking had earned Blaine almost as many enemies as friends, and a sizable number of delegates felt that he had no chance of being elected.

Blaine knew that he was unlikely to be nominated without a long and bitter fight at the convention. He also knew that the Republicans' best chance of unseating the Democratic President lay in finding a candidate who could unite the party. Recent Republican administrations—those of Ulysses S. Grant, Rutherford B. Hayes, and Chester A. Arthur—had been

James G. Blaine of Maine was a powerful Republican who never succeeded in becoming President, despite many attempts. He threw his support behind Harrison, helped him get elected, and then served under him as secretary of state. (Library of Congress.)

either troubled or uninspired. The Republicans needed to confront the nation's voters with a strong, positive candidate. As a war hero and former senator with few political enemies, Harrison seemed ideal.

Blaine was a wily and shrewd politician. He decided not to try for the Republican nomination, because he knew that his political career would be over if he ran again for the presidency and lost. Just before the convention started, Blaine withdrew his name from consideration. He let it be known, however, that he favored Harrison as the candidate. Although he might not be strong enough to win the nomination, Blaine was still a very powerful Republican. His support meant that Harrison stood a good chance of winning the nomination. Nevertheless, he had strong rivals: John Sherman of Ohio, Judge Walter Q. Gresham of Indiana, Chauncey Depew of New York, Russell Alger of Michigan, and William B. Allison of Iowa.

THE ELECTION OF 1888

Louis T. Michener, an Indiana attorney and friend of Harrison's, was the head of the Hoosier delegates to the Republican National Convention. He tried to arrange matters in Harrison's favor by creating a repeat of the 1880 convention, at which James Garfield had been nominated. Michener figured that if all the other rivals were left to fight it out in the early ballots, none of them would win the necessary majority. Then Harrison could step in and scoop up the votes as everybody's *second* choice.

Michener's plan worked. Sherman led on the first ballot, but each of the other contenders received enough votes to keep Sherman short of a majority. After each vote, party leaders and delegates met to argue and compromise. Soon most of them agreed that if their own favorites could not be nominated, they would support Harrison. As a result, Harrison reached second place by the fourth ballot. On the eighth ballot, he received a majority of the votes. Benjamin Harrison was the party's candidate for President.

For Vice-President, the Republicans nominated Levi P. Morton of New York, who had served in the U.S. House of Representatives and as minister (something like a present-day ambassador) to France. The party's platform—the principles and plans a political party presents to voters—included civil service reform, expansion of the Navy, and statehood for the territories. It also included federal aid to education, better pensions for veterans, and changes in certain taxes.

The Front-Porch Campaign

Political contests have always contained a certain amount of what is sometimes called "mudslinging"—that is, insults between candidates and their supporters, or damaging rumors about the candidates. Some 19th-century campaigns were especially noteworthy for the amount of mud that was slung. But the campaign of 1888 was a model of gentlemanly behavior. One observer said, "I cannot recall another presidential contest that was conducted on both sides with greater dignity and decency than that between Cleveland and Harrison."

Part of this dignity came from the fact that neither man campaigned hard for himself. Instead, both of them followed a tradition that was beginning to seem rather old-fashioned by 1888. It was a tradition among presidential candidates of letting other people do most of the campaigning for them. Like most incumbents—people already in office who are running for re-election—Cleveland carried on with his presidential activities and made no special effort to go out and win votes. As for Harrison, he took the advice of his campaign manager, Matthew Quay of Pennsylvania, and limited him-

One gimmick of Harrison's presidential campaign was this so-called "campaign ball." It was 14 feet across and 42 feet around. Supporters of "gallant Ben" rolled the ball across hundreds of miles to drum up votes. (Library of Congress.)

self to speech-making from the steps of his home in Indianapolis. As political clubs, voters' groups, veterans' organizations, and other delegations paraded past his house almost every day, he would deliver a carefully prepared address to each group. All told, more than 300,000 people visited Harrison at his home, and he made more than 80 speeches. This low-keyed, domestic approach to politicking soon earned Harrison's campaign the nickname "front-porch campaign." Outside Indiana, the Harrison campaign was headed by Blaine.

The election in November was very close. Cleveland received 5,540,329 popular votes to Harrison's 5,439,853. But a U.S. President is actually elected by the electoral college, which does not always coincide with the popular vote.

The election of 1888 was one of several elections in American history in which the candidate chosen by popular vote was not the candidate elected by the electoral college. Harrison won 233 electoral votes, while Cleveland won only 168. When he received the good news by telegram, a jubilant but reserved Harrison, now 55 years old, offered a prayer of thanks for his victory. He also prayed for strength and guidance during his coming presidency.

Celebrating a Century

The United States had many 100-year anniversaries during the 19th century. In 1876 it celebrated the 100th anniversary of the Declaration of Independence. In 1887 it celebrated the 100th anniversary of the Constitution. And in 1889 Harrison was inaugurated President on the 100th anniversary of the first presidential inauguration, that of George Washington.

March 4, 1889, was a gray and rainy day, with a cold wind. But foul weather could not keep away the crowds that lined Pennsylvania Avenue and other thoroughfares of the nation's capital to watch their President being inaugurated. Storekeepers and hotelkeepers offered lookout spots at their windows for six dollars a person. The cheering during the morning became a deafening roar at one o'clock in the afternoon, when Cleveland and Harrison took their places on a roofed outdoor stage. After Harrison's oath of office and inaugural speech, the presidential party made its way to the White House.

Later in the afternoon there was a tremendous parade. Hundreds of military regiments and marching clubs paraded

Harrison's inaugural ball, held in the Pension Building (shown at lower left), was a grand and sparkling scene. More than 12,000 people danced and feasted in celebration of their centennial President. (Library of Congress.)

past a reviewing stand, and the President raised his hat to each one. Among the thousands of people in the grand procession were more than 40,000 who had witnessed the inauguration of William Henry Harrison on that same spot nearly 50 years before. Flags, banners, posters, and colorful umbrellas were waved; bands played; horses pranced. In the evening, more than 12,000 danced and enjoyed a splendid feast at the inaugural ball. On that day, America celebrated not only the inauguration of its new President, but also a century of presidential history.

IN THE WHITE HOUSE

The Harrisons brought a large family to the White House. In addition to Benjamin and Carrie, the household included the aging Dr. John Scott, Carrie's father, who was 90 years old when Harrison became President. Mamie accompanied her parents in order to help her mother with the heavy task of being Washington's official hostess. She brought her two small children, Benjamin McKee and Mary Lodge McKee. Her husband, Bob McKee, spent part of his time in Indianapolis and part of it at the White House with his family. Russell Harrison divided his time between the White House and his business concerns in Montana, where he now ran a newspaper as well as a ranch. But his wife, Mary, and their daughter, Marthena, lived in the White House.

It was the custom of the time for unmarried or widowed women to live with their married sisters. Accordingly, the Harrison household also included Carrie's older sister, whose husband had died some years before. This sister died during the Harrisons' first year in the White House, but her 30-year-old daughter, Mary Lord Dimmick, continued to be part of

Among the rooms that Carrie cleaned and redecorated at the White House was her husband's bedroom. For privacy, he sometimes worked at the writing table there instead of in his office. (Library of Congress.)

the family. She helped Carrie manage the household, the large staff of servants, and the children. Mary Dimmick was to play an unexpected and somewhat controversial role in Harrison's future.

At first, the Harrisons had some difficulty settling down in their new home. Besides the confusion of such a large family, the President and Carrie had made the mistake of inviting all their friends and acquaintances to visit them at the White House. For some months after the inauguration, life for the Harrisons seemed to consist of a steady stream of callers, all eager to tell the folks back home about their visit with the President.

Redecorating the Executive Mansion

Eventually, however, things settled down. Then, like many First Ladies before her, Carrie set about the task of cleaning, redecorating, and reorganizing the White House. Although some earlier residents—most recently, President Chester Arthur—had decorated the mansion, the basics of plumbing and carpentry had been overlooked for many years. Carrie wanted to get rid of the mildew and mold on some of the walls, to repair rotten stairwells, and in general to give the White House a brand-new, healthier look. To do so, she obtained a grant of $35,000 from Congress.

Carrie's first step was to have the old building's flourishing populations of insects and mice exterminated. Then she ordered a complete scrubbing and repainting of the entire structure. She had new plumbing installed, adding several bathrooms in the process. She also had electricity installed, but she was so frightened of this newfangled feature that at first she refused to turn off the light switches. Thus, the White House windows would shine brightly all night long until an engineer demonstrated to Carrie that it was safe to touch the switches. Finally, she completed a job that had been started by President Arthur—emptying out cupboards and closets full of musty old clothing and documents that had been left behind by generations of earlier Presidents.

Once this massive cleaning, restoration, and reconstruction job was finished, Carrie began to enjoy White House life. It was she who, in 1889, started the custom of putting up a large Christmas tree in the White House. And now she put her artistic talent to use by making floral arrangements of orchids and other blooms to beautify the executive mansion. She also conducted classes for the ladies of Washington in the popular hobby of painting pictures on china plates. During Harrison's presidency, a group of women whose ancestors had fought in the American Revolution decided to form a national patriotic organization. Carrie was elected the first president of this group, which was called the Daughters of the American Revolution (DAR).

Harrison, too, enjoyed White House life once the confusion of settling in was over. He adored his grandchildren, especially young Benjamin, who was called Baby McKee. He was frequently photographed with one or more of the youngsters on his lap—or tugging at his long, full beard. With his twinkling blue eyes, ruddy complexion, white whiskers, and plump body, Harrison must have looked to his grandchildren very much like the traditional figure of Santa Claus, or St. Nicholas.

The President also liked to take long walks or buggy rides around the city. One of his favorite pastimes was to drive his prized Kentucky thoroughbred horses and his dark green buggy into Maryland or Virginia. Once out of sight of the capital, Harrison would take over the reins from his coachman.

The family's religious life continued in the capital. Daily

Harrison's large White House family included Mamie and her two children (left) and Russell's wife, Mary, and their daughter (right). The three small children often appeared in newspaper pictures. Harrison's favorite, little Benjamin McKee, was nicknamed "Baby McKee." (Library of Congress.)

prayers were led by Harrison or Dr. Scott, and the family attended a new Presbyterian church. Sundays were days of prayer and quiet. At other times, however, the social life of the White House was quite lively. The games and pranks of the children were often reported in the gossip columns of the newspapers. The younger Harrisons encouraged dancing at formal parties and receptions for the first time since such gaiety had been banished by the wife of President Polk years before.

Harrison's Cabinet

Of course, most of Harrison's time and energy were spent on more serious matters. One of his first concerns, as of every President, was to appoint a Cabinet, the group of advisors and administrators who oversee the day-to-day operations of the government. Harrison initially appointed six lawyers and two businessmen to his Cabinet.

William H.H. Miller, Harrison's law partner, was made attorney general. He won praise for his fairness in selecting federal judges on the basis of their merits, not of their political ties.

Benjamin F. Tracy of New York was Harrison's secretary of the Navy. He continued a program of modernization and enlargement of the U.S. Navy that had been started under President Arthur. Sometimes called "the father of the modern Navy," Tracy supported an ambitious program of shipbuilding that helped make the U.S. Navy a world power by the beginning of the 20th century.

John Wanamaker of Pennsylvania was the postmaster general. The owner of a famous department store in Philadelphia, Wanamaker was known to be a shrewd and practical businessman. He made several recommendations that were eventually adopted by the Post Office Department, including the rural free delivery (RFD) program for country dwellers and the parcel post system for mailing packages.

John W. Noble of Missouri served as secretary of the interior. One of his important accomplishments was to organize some of the remaining frontier land into the Oklahoma Territory and open it to settlers in 1889. Another was to get Congress to pass a law that allowed Presidents to set aside timberlands as forest reserves where loggers and farmers could not cut trees. Harrison then created reserves totaling 13 million acres.

Jeremiah M. Rusk of Wisconsin was the secretary of agriculture. His most significant contribution was to begin federal inspection of meat that was being sold to other countries. European nations periodically claimed that American meat exports carried disease (such claims were almost always untrue but were spread by the meat producers of rival nations). The program begun by Rusk was the first step in fighting these accusations and improving the country's meat trade.

Harrison had two secretaries of the treasury. The first, William Windom of Minnesota, was a longtime friend and advisor. He died in 1891 and was replaced by Charles Foster of Ohio, another of Harrison's friends.

Two men served as secretary of war under Harrison. The first was Redfield Proctor of Vermont, who resigned in 1891 to accept a seat in the U.S. Senate. The second was Stephen B. Elkins of West Virginia, a wealthy factory owner who became a U.S. senator after Harrison's administration.

MATTERS OF STATE

The secretary of state is usually considered the most important Cabinet official. It is his responsibility to make sure that relationships between the United States and other nations run smoothly and to protect U.S. interests around the world. Many of the early secretaries of state went on to become Presidents (Jefferson, Madison, Monroe, John Quincy Adams, Van Buren, and Buchanan), and the tradition of power and significance that went with this office continued in Harrison's time.

Harrison had two secretaries of state. He awarded the post first to James Blaine, the Republican leader from Maine.

Blaine had served as secretary of state in the Garfield and Arthur administrations. He resigned his Cabinet position in June of 1892 because of poor health, and he died the following year. His replacement in Harrison's Cabinet was John W. Foster of Indiana.

Both Blaine and Foster were ambitious and active men who favored a policy of national growth called expansionism. This way of thinking was shared by many Americans in the second half of the 19th century. It held that the United States should expand its territories where possible and should also become a leader in world politics and trade. Expansionists felt that a large, modern, prosperous country such as the United States had a responsibility to help other, less fortunate nations manage their affairs. Sometimes, of course, that "help" was not really desired by the other nations. Nevertheless, Harrison's administration marked an era when the United States was being recognized beyond its own borders as a major world power. The greatest successes of Harrison's presidency involved foreign affairs.

The Pan-American Conference

One of these successes was a project that Secretary Blaine had been trying to complete since Garfield's election in 1880. This was a conference of representatives from all the independent nations of Central and South America. It was called the International Conference of American States, but it and later such conferences are usually grouped together under the name Pan-American conferences (from the Greek word *pan*, meaning "all"). Blaine believed that the nations of the Western Hemisphere should cooperate to promote trade and to prevent war. He also believed that the United States should take the role of leader in these cooperative ventures.

After a decade of effort, Blaine finally received congressional approval to hold a Pan-American Conference in 1889. With much fanfare and publicity, representatives from 18 Western Hemisphere nations held meetings in New York and Washington. Then they were escorted on a tour of factories and farms in the Midwest and South. Although this first Pan-American Conference did not accomplish as much as Blaine had hoped, it did result in a few favorable agreements on import and export taxes with some of the Latin American nations.

Of more lasting importance, the first Pan-American Conference established a basis for future discussion, negotiation, and cooperation among the nations of the hemisphere. For a few weeks at least, it gave the republics of North, Central, and South America a chance to think of themselves as neighbors, rather than as rivals or enemies. This was Blaine's greatest achievement as secretary of state.

Peaceful Solutions

Secretary of State Blaine also helped Harrison reach peaceful solutions to some nasty international problems. Thanks in large part to Blaine's sound advice and smooth diplomacy, the Harrison administration was very effective in its handling of foreign affairs.

Two violent incidents that occurred during Harrison's presidency almost involved the U.S. in wars. One of them took place in New Orleans, where many Italians had settled or were living and working temporarily. Some of the people of New Orleans believed that the Italians were responsible for a crime wave in the city. Without waiting for the police and the courts to determine the facts, a crowd of angry citizens

President Harrison helped settle an international dispute over the fur seals of the Pribilof Islands, near Alaska. Hunting by the British had nearly exterminated the seals by the 1890s, but Harrison persuaded Great Britain to agree to a plan to limit hunting. (Library of Congress.)

took the law into their own hands and murdered three Italians. The government and people of Italy were so furious that, for several months, there was a possibility of war between the two nations. But Blaine and Harrison calmed the Italians by making sure that the murders were publicly investigated and the ringleaders punished.

The other war threat concerned the South American nation of Chile. Relations between the two countries took a bad turn when Chilean revolutionaries bought a shipload of weapons in California and tried to smuggle them into Chile to overthrow the government. Several U.S. Navy ships chased the vessel carrying the weapons all the way to the coast of Chile. After catching the ship, the Americans forced the Chileans to turn over the guns, claiming that they had been smuggled out of the United States illegally. American ships then remained in the Pacific waters off Chile.

Eventually, however, the Chilean rebels succeeded in taking over the government. Because the country's new leaders resented what they considered to have been Yankee interference in their business, Americans became unpopular in Chile. When a crew of American seamen foolishly went ashore at the Chilean port of Valparaiso, a brawl with some local people resulted in the deaths of two U.S. sailors. The American public demanded vengeance, and many people wanted Harrison to declare war on Chile.

The President himself called the killings "savage, brutal, and unprovoked" and was inclined to consider them an act of war. But Blaine truly wanted to preserve the peace. Indeed, he seemed to be the only member of the Cabinet or Congress who was not eager to go to war to avenge national honor. He managed to persuade the revolutionary government of Chile to issue a formal apology to Washington and to pay $75,000 to the families of the slain sailors. Harrison and the Congress pronounced that they were satisfied, and the crisis ended.

South Seas Adventures

Two affairs of state during Harrison's administration concerned islands in the Pacific Ocean. These exotic, lush, far-off places had been brought to the attention of the American public by the novels and stories of writers like Robert Louis Stevenson and Herman Melville. The Pacific islands in the South Seas had a very practical value in addition to their beauty and glamour. They were not rich in natural resources, but they did provide ideal places for ships cruising the Pacific to take on fuel and other supplies. In addition, agents stationed in outposts on the islands could keep track of the movements of navies and commercial fleets around the Pacific. As a result, toward the end of the 19th century the Pacific islands began to fall under the control of European nations – and the United States did not intend to be left out.

Germany hoped to establish a strong naval force in the Pacific and wanted to obtain the Samoan Islands as a military and supply base. But the United States wanted to limit Germany's power in the Pacific and also wanted to take over the Samoan Islands for itself. Ships from both nations' navies maneuvered menacingly for a few months and almost came to war.

Blaine and Harrison arranged a conference in Berlin, Germany, to decide the fate of the Samoan Islands. The Samoans, however, were not consulted. Eventually, the western part of the island group came under German control and the eastern part under American control. Today, Western Samoa is an independent island nation, while the rest of the island group, called American Samoa, remains a U.S. territory.

America's other Pacific adventure took place north of Samoa, in the Hawaiian Islands. In 1893 the United States made an attempt to annex Hawaii – that is, to make the islands officially a part of American territory. The annexation attempt failed, however. Harrison was annoyed and regarded this failure as the one black mark against his administration's foreign policy.

The Last Queen

When the Hawaiian Islands were discovered by the British explorer Captain James Cook in 1778, they were ruled by kings and queens. For the next century, while Europeans landed on the islands and claimed various trading rights, Hawaii remained independent under its royal rulers. But as early as 1845, some Americans proposed the annexation (formal acquisition) of Hawaii. Later, Americans even prevented the French and the British from taking over the islands. By the late 19th century, many of Hawaii's rulers were willing to have the islands become closely associated with the United States. By the 1880s, the United States had established a naval fueling station at Pearl Harbor, on the island of Oahu.

In 1874 a king named Kalakaua came to the Hawaiian throne. During Harrison's administration, King Kalakaua started to reverse the pro-American trend. He began a policy of returning Hawaii to its traditional way of life, including the ancient privilege of the king to rule without question and with the power of life and death over his subjects. He also wanted to reduce the number of foreigners in Hawaii, perhaps to keep them out entirely.

Some Hawaiians welcomed this return to an earlier tradition, but others wanted to retain the democratic privileges they had gained under the influence of the foreigners. There were several rebellions before Kalakaua's rule ended in 1891. The throne then went to his sister Liliuokalani, who continued her brother's policies under the slogan "Hawaii for the Hawaiians."

Liliuokalani was destined to be the last queen of Hawaii. In January of 1893, rebellious Hawaiians, supported by the United States, deposed Queen Liliuokalani—that is, removed her from the throne. Her place as ruler was taken by a temporary council of ministers. Harrison and his new secretary of state, John Foster, wanted to take advantage of Hawaii's internal troubles to annex the islands.

Unfortunately for Harrison's plans, the idea of annexation was resisted by both some Hawaiians and some American congressmen. Hawaii governed itself as an independent republic under U.S. protection for a few more years. Not until 1900 did Hawaii officially become an American territory. It became the 50th state—and the only U.S. state to have had its own kings and queens—in 1959.

Chapter 9

Money Matters

Harrison was busy on the home front, too. However, his domestic policies were not, on the whole, as successful as his foreign ones. In one area, though, Harrison was more successful than any other President. Six territories were admitted to statehood during his administration, more than during any other President's term of office. They were North Dakota (1889), South Dakota (1889), Montana (1889), Washington (1889), Idaho (1890), and Wyoming (1890). Having strongly favored statehood for the western territories while he was a member of the U.S. Senate, Harrison took great pride in presiding over the addition of six new states.

Harrison also appointed four justices to the U.S. Supreme Court. David J. Brewer of Kansas is remembered for upholding a law that said that women could not be forced to work more than 10 hours a day. Henry Brown of Michigan was an expert on admiralty law (the body of law that governs navigation, rights to the sea, and shipping). This was a useful asset in an age of increasing sea traffic. He and fellow justice George Shiras of Pennsylvania, also a Harrison appointee, disagreed over the federal income tax law. Shiras' vote overturned the law, and Brown criticized this majority opinion. The country was without an income tax for only a few years, however, as the law was restored within a short time. Harrison's fourth appointment to the court had little chance to distinguish himself. He was Howell E. Jackson of Tennessee, a Democrat. Harrison appointed him to avoid criticism for selecting only Republicans, but Jackson died of tuberculosis after only two years on the bench.

HARRISON'S FOUR ACTS

The years of Harrison's presidency were years of growing economic trouble and social unrest in the United States. Large corporations had begun to flourish, and they joined together in larger and richer business associations called trusts and holding companies. Smaller companies found it impossible to compete with these industrial giants, and small businessmen and farmers resented the control that the millionaires of "Big Business" seemed to have over the nation. On top of this problem, the number of poor people was growing. Their poverty fueled the fires of resentment toward the government and the big corporations.

Harrison's administration pushed through Congress four important acts that were intended to help solve some of the economic problems facing the country. All four became law in 1890. That same year, many Democrats were elected to the Senate and the House of Representatives. With an uncooperative Congress, Harrison was unable to pass any significant legislation after 1890.

Dependent and Disability Pensions Act

Harrison had always favored giving war veterans the largest possible pensions, and he was extremely pleased when Congress approved the Dependent and Disability Pensions Act.

This law granted a pension, or cash income for life, to any Civil War veteran who was too disabled to work, even if the disability was not caused by the war. In other words, if a veteran had been injured in a fall from a horse 10 years after the war ended and could not work, he was now entitled to receive a pension. The act also gave an income to the widows or orphan children of veterans.

When this act became law, one congressman estimated that by 1893 it would cost the government $159 million to pay the pensions, as opposed to $88 million in 1889. Harrison did not care. To him, aid to veterans was both necessary and noble.

Sherman Antitrust Act

Sponsored by Senator John Sherman of Ohio, the Sherman Antitrust Act was the government's first attempt to control the large corporate trusts that had begun to dominate American business life. These corporate organizations sometimes cooperated with each other to raise their profits. For example, all the railroad companies would get together and agree to keep prices at a certain level. Because they monopolized, or controlled, whole sections of the economy, these arrangements were sometimes called monopolies.

The Sherman Antitrust Act made it a crime to engage in a trust or monopoly that would control trade. Anyone convicted of being in such a trust could be fined or sent to jail. But the act had a number of loopholes, so it was not as strong against trusts as its backers hoped it would be. Nevertheless, it was an important first step in the war on unfair business practices. It provided the groundwork for more vigorous antitrust legislation during the presidencies of Theodore Roosevelt and William Howard Taft.

McKinley Tariff Act

William McKinley, a congressman from Ohio, sponsored an act to reform tariffs, the taxes on goods brought into or sent out of the country. Tariffs had been a troublesome issue in American politics and economics for years. But with the McKinley Tariff Act, the country got more than it expected.

The act set the average tariff rate at 48 percent of the cost of the imported goods. This was the highest the tariff rate had ever been in peacetime. It was intended to help U.S. industries compete with imported products, but the overall effect was to raise the price paid by the average citizen for all kinds of goods. The act placed high tariffs on some classes of products that were not even manufactured in the United States. These imports became very costly even though no American industries were being protected. At the same time, sugar, which was produced in quantity in Louisiana, was placed on the tariff-free list, which meant that imported sugar could be sold cheaply. But to help the farmers of Louisiana, the U.S. government paid them two cents for every pound of sugar they produced. This money was paid by taxpayers, who would have preferred to buy the cheaper sugar. Both farmers and importers raised their prices, and sugar ended up costing more, not less. The McKinley Tariff Act was generally judged to be a poor piece of legislation, and it hurt the Republicans in state and local elections. It was replaced by a new tariff act in 1894.

Sherman Silver Purchase Act

The fourth major act passed during Harrison's administration was also sponsored by Ohioan John Sherman. It concerned another pressing economic issue: the question of gold, silver, and paper money. Two groups of people wanted more

Tariffs

Because most countries want to make it easy for other countries to buy their goods and products, buyers or shippers rarely have to pay tariffs on materials that are being exported, or sold outside the country where the items are made. Tariffs are more often applied to incoming goods or products. That is, the importer of a product from a foreign country must pay the U.S. government a fee in order to bring it into the United States. If the importer is a merchant who wants to sell the product, he will add the cost of the tariff to the price he charges for the item. In the end, the consumer pays more for imported goods that are subject to a tariff.

At various times, the United States has assigned different tariffs to different classes of goods. The most common reason for setting high tariffs is called protectionism. This means that a high tariff is imposed on foreign goods in order to protect American companies and workers that make the same goods. For example, if a railway car made in Mexico was significantly cheaper than one made in the United States, soon the railway car manufacturers of the United States would be out of business. Therefore, the government may decide to protect the U.S. railway car industry by imposing a high tariff on foreign-made railway cars.

If the U.S. wants to sell its products in another country, it may lower the tariff on goods imported from that country. This action is called reciprocity. It allows two nations to import from each other without a high tariff on either side. On the other hand, the U.S. may raise its tariffs on products from certain countries in order to punish those countries for having high tariffs of their own.

One objection to tariffs is that they limit trade. Some economists feel that trade between nations should flow freely, with buyers and sellers charging whatever they can, and without the artificial price levels that are set by tariffs. In the example of the railway cars, these economists would claim that it is the right of the railways to buy the cheapest possible railway cars, no matter where they come from. If the railways cannot do this—in other words, if they have to pay more to buy American-made cars—they will simply charge the passengers more for their tickets, and the economy will suffer.

The debate between supporters of free trade and supporters of protectionism continues today, and it will probably never end. It was one of the most hotly argued issues of Harrison's day. Everyone had an opinion on the tariff question. In general, the Democrats stood for free trade and the Republicans stood for protectionism. In choosing Harrison over Cleveland in 1888, the nation seemed to be speaking up in support of a strong protective tariff.

silver money to be coined. One group consisted of mine owners, bankers, and businessmen who owned or controlled the silver-producing companies in the West. They wanted the amount of silver currency in the country to increase so that they could sell their silver ore to the government.

The other prosilver group consisted of farmers, mostly in the Midwest. The 1880s had been a time of low prices for farm products, and many farmers were in deep financial trouble. They felt that an increase in the amount of currency in the country would mean more money for everyone and would therefore help them avoid bankruptcy or additional financial losses.

To please these two groups, Congress passed the Sherman Silver Purchase Act in 1890. This law required the U.S. Treasury to buy 4.5 million ounces of silver each month — almost the complete output of the nation's silver mines! But the government paid for the silver with notes, or paper money, that could be cashed in for gold. Many of the miners and others who received the government notes promptly cashed them in. Within a very short time, the Treasury's reserve supply of gold — the supply that backed up the value of all American currency — was seriously reduced. Furthermore, the addition of lots of silver money to the nation's currency meant that more money existed, but the purchasing power of each dollar went down. Like the McKinley Tariff Act, the Sherman Silver Purchase Act remained in force for only a few years. It was repealed in 1895.

Civil Service Reform

The movement to reform the civil service and to end the practice of patronage gained strength throughout the 1880s. Reformers had hoped for support from Harrison. After all, while he was a senator he had voted in favor of the Pendleton Act — the first civil service reform act — in 1883. After being elected President, however, the reformers criticized Harrison for giving many public service positions to his friends and to people who had helped him get elected. One case that attracted much attention was that of William Wallace, Harrison's old law partner from Indianapolis.

The head of the Civil Service Commission at this time was Theodore Roosevelt of New York, who was deeply committed to reform. Roosevelt, though, did everything in a splashy and energetic way. He made sweeping accusations about Harrison's appointments, but the facts did not always support Roosevelt's criticism. After Harrison had appointed Will Wallace as city postmaster of Indianapolis, Roosevelt charged that Wallace was not executing his duties properly. But an investigation showed that Wallace had not done anything wrong, and he was permitted to keep the job.

Roosevelt's aggressive manner—as well as the threat to their patronage jobs—caused many Republicans to turn against the idea of civil service reform. President Harrison, too, proved less of a reformer than Roosevelt and others had hoped. He felt he could not afford to turn too many powerful Republicans against him. Roosevelt called Harrison "a cold-blooded, narrow-minded, prejudiced, obstinate, timid old psalm-singing Indianapolis politician." And reformer William Dudley Foulke said, "Four years ago our civil service reformers in Indiana were all supporting the Republican Party . . . were all active supporters of Mr. Harrison. After four years of his Administration they are now for Cleveland."

THE ELECTION OF 1892

By the time the presidential election year of 1892 rolled around, Harrison had lost ground with the public and with his party. People were unhappy with the high prices brought about by the McKinley Tariff Act. Moreover, there was a general feeling that Harrison did not have a solid plan for keeping the economy steady—and, in truth, he did not. In addition, many voters were appalled at the amount of money spent by Congress during Harrison's administration. His was the first billion-dollar Congress in American history, with almost 1 billion 27 million dollars in appropriations needed to carry out congressional expenditures. For these reasons, Americans were less enthusiastic about Harrison than they had been a few years before.

The Republicans, however, did not have another candidate to propose. Blaine, who had been a key figure at so many Republican conventions, was too ill to consider running again. In fact, he died before Harrison left office. Having no other choice, the Republicans nominated Harrison at their national convention in Minneapolis. Throughout the summer campaign, they tried to emphasize his successes in foreign policy.

President Harrison had followed a strict policy of "being his own boss," as observers at the time called it. This meant that he did not always follow the advice or suggestions of some influential Republican Party leaders. This strong-minded, independent attitude was admirable in some ways, but it resulted in the loss of support from people who had backed him four years earlier. One loss that hurt Harrison was that of Matthew Quay of Pennsylvania, who had managed his campaign in 1888. Quay was angry at Harrison for not giving him a more important role in the administration, and he refused to act again as campaign manager.

Harrison's Double Loss

The Democrats nominated Grover Cleveland, who had preceded Harrison in the White House. The campaign was a quiet one; some called it dull. But it took a tragic turn for Harrison when Carrie fell ill in the autumn. Her health had been delicate for nearly a decade, and she was subject to frequent colds. This time, however, her condition was more serious; she had tuberculosis. She died on October 25, just two weeks before the election.

A hopeful newspaper cartoon of August 1892 shows a muscular Harrison getting the best of an out-of-shape Grover Cleveland in a boxing ring. But at the polls a few months later, the champion was Cleveland. (Library of Congress.)

The 59-year-old Harrison was devastated at the loss of his wife of nearly 40 years. He even wondered whether his insistence on the stressful life of a Washington politician had weakened her health by bringing her to the damp, often uncomfortable capital to live. He was so deeply sunk in grief that he seemed scarcely to care when the election results came in and he learned that he had lost. Grover Cleveland was to be the next President, and Harrison would go down in history as the only President to be preceded and followed in office by the same person.

Chapter **10**

Retirement

Harrison said that his failure to be re-elected brought him "no personal disappointments or griefs." He told a friend, "Indeed, after the heavy blow that the death of my wife dealt me, I do not think I could stand the strain a re-election would have brought."

Yet it saddened Harrison to see the Republican Party, to which he had dedicated his entire adult life, lose to the Democrats. And he was sorry to know that some of the landmarks of his administration—the McKinley Tariff Act, for example—would be undone by the next administration. Although he never said so, it must have been painful for a proud man with a distinguished heritage to realize that he was not popular enough to win a second term.

RETURN TO INDIANAPOLIS

Harrison's last day in Washington was March 4, 1893, the day of Cleveland's inauguration. The outgoing President noted that it was a "fearfully bad" day, colder than the day of his own inauguration, and that it snowed. Harrison politely attended the inauguration ceremony, then he was escorted to the train station by the members of his Cabinet. If his departure from Washington made him downhearted, however, he was cheered by the warm welcome he received in Indianapolis, where applauding crowds rushed to shake his hand. "I made no mistake in coming home at once," Harrison said to his son, Russell. "There are no friends like the old ones."

Harrison's first task was to make himself at home in his old house. He had a new stable built and a new porch added. Then he tackled the chore of unpacking his china, books, and other possessions—a chore that Carrie had always done with pleasure. Soon his daughter, Mamie, and her two children came to stay with him, and their company lifted his spirits. The children's pet goat and burro grazed on the Harrison lawn and quickly became a joke with the neighbors.

Work and Travel

Harrison returned to law practice, taking only selected cases and serving as an advisor. He told his clients that he would make court appearances only in emergency cases, and he charged a high fee. Yet he had as much work as he wanted.

Harrison also made speaking appearances. In December, at the request of his friend and former Cabinet member John Wanamaker, he delivered a speech to a club in Philadelphia. In the spring of 1894, he delivered a series of six lectures on constitutional law at Stanford University in California for a fee of $25,000. He was offered a professorship in law at the University of Chicago, but he turned it down. He was comfortably wealthy and did not wish to be tied to a strict teaching schedule. He preferred to pick and choose his law cases and to write magazine articles.

One writing project was a series of nine very short articles about America and its governmental institutions for *The*

Ladies' Home Journal, for which Harrison was paid $5,000. In addition, Harrison enjoyed frequent visits to friends on the East Coast, often staying in New Jersey resort communities where he and Carrie had vacationed during his presidency.

A New Marriage

At Christmas of 1895, Harrison made a surprising announcement to his family. He told Russell and Mamie that he had fallen in love and planned to marry again. His bride would be their cousin, Mary Lord Dimmick, who had lived with the family in the White House. Harrison was 62; Mary was 37.

The announcement startled and angered Harrison's children. Russell and Mamie opposed the marriage because the bride was 25 years younger than their father and because she was a relative. But Harrison had grown very fond of Mary, and he hated and feared loneliness. In his usual firm way, he refused to consider changing his plans. Both of his children then told him that they would not attend the wedding and that he could expect to see less of them and of his grandchildren in the future. Yet Harrison wrote to Russell, "It is natural that a man's former children should not be pleased ordinarily, with a second marriage . . . . But my life now, and much more as I grow older, is and will be a very lonely one and I cannot go on as now."

The wedding took place on April 6, 1896, at St. Thomas Episcopal Church in New York City. Benjamin Tracy, Harrison's former secretary of the Navy, was the best man. In addition to several other Cabinet members, the three dozen guests also included Levi Morton, who had been the groom's Vice-President.

Harrison and his bride settled in Indianapolis, where they had a happy marriage and a busy social life. Harrison was

*Mary Lord Dimmick, Carrie's niece, married Harrison in 1896.
The marriage brought happiness and a new baby daughter into
Harrison's later years, but it angered Russell and Mamie, who
withdrew from their father.* (Library of Congress.)

thrilled when, in February of 1897, a daughter was born. He and Mary named her Elizabeth. Many years later, Elizabeth was to marry the grandson of her father's old political ally, James G. Blaine of Maine.

FINAL YEARS

From time to time, Harrison's friends tried to entice him back into politics. As dissatisfaction with Cleveland's second administration grew, some Republicans felt that Harrison should run for President again in 1896. But he never considered such a course and firmly turned down all the hints and offers that came his way. Harrison did, however, campaign on behalf of the Republican candidate, William McKinley, and was pleased when McKinley was elected.

The biggest legal case of Harrison's later career involved politics. It concerned a boundary dispute between the South American nation of Venezuela and the neighboring colony of British Guiana. The dispute was to be settled at a hearing before an international commission in Paris. The Venezuelans hired Harrison as one of their legal advisors.

The case was complicated, and Harrison was required to search records covering several centuries of settlement and colonization. He began his preparation of the case in 1897 and continued until the hearing took place in 1899. Harrison's handling of the case was widely admired as a masterpiece of detail and thoroughness. He wrote an 800-page report and delivered more than 25 hours of testimony in five days. But in spite of his well-presented case, British Guiana was awarded about 90 percent of the territory that Venezuela wanted. Harrison was disappointed, but he took satisfaction in the knowledge that he had done his best, and Venezuela was grateful for his efforts.

After the hearing, Harrison took a short European tour with his wife and then returned to Indianapolis. The Venezuela case was his last large project. After his return to Indianapolis, he did not again leave home for long.

Illness and Death

In March of 1901, Harrison became ill with influenza. His sickness worsened rapidly, and on March 12 he fell into unconsciousness. He died the next day, at the age of 67.

For several days, the body of the only Hoosier President lay in a flag-draped casket in the Indiana statehouse. Thousands of mourners passed by to pay their last respects. Harrison's funeral was held at the First Presbyterian Church, the same church he had joined upon moving to Indianapolis so many years before. He was buried at Carrie's side in the city's Crown Hill Cemetery. The bulk of his fortune, worth about $400,000, was left to Mary and Elizabeth. Although he had had little contact with his older children following his remarriage, he left a small sum to Mamie and a similar sum to be used for the education of Russell's children.

Harrison did not leave a legacy of great leadership like those left by Washington, Jefferson, and Lincoln. He is not remembered for guiding the country through a war or other desperate crisis, like Franklin D. Roosevelt. Nor is he remembered for changing the course of American history by bold actions and grand plans, like John F. Kennedy. Instead, he is remembered as a man of stern dignity, high intelligence, and unquestioned honesty, who carried out the duties of his office faithfully, although without great vision. His biggest gift to the party he served was to restore its good name after a series of incompetent Presidents had given the Republicans a bad reputation. His biggest service to the nation was to show that honesty, high ideals, and integrity belonged in the White House.

Perhaps the best summary of Harrison's many admirable personal qualities came from James Whitcomb Riley, the popular Hoosier poet, who delivered a speech of tribute at Harrison's funeral. "One of the characteristics of General Harrison always commanded my profound respect—his fearless independence and stand for what he believed to be right and just," Riley said. "A fearless man inwardly commands respect, and above everything else Harrison was fearless and just." Harrison may have failed to win the nation's lasting affection, but he certainly could claim its respect.

Bibliography

Sievers, Harry J. *Benjamin Harrison: Hoosier Warrior.* Chicago: Henry Regnery, 1952.

Sievers, Harry J. *Benjamin Harrison: Hoosier Statesman.* New York: University Publishers, 1957.

Sievers, Harry J. *Benjamin Harrison: Hoosier President.* New York: Bobbs-Merrill, 1968.

Taken together, these three books are the only modern biography of Benjamin Harrison. Several accounts of his life and his family were written during his lifetime, but they are brief and not very factual. Sievers' first book covers the years from Harrison's birth through the Civil War. The second book covers the years from 1865 to his presidential election in 1888. The third and final book deals with his presidency and retirement. All three contain many quotations from Harrison's letters, speeches, and writings.

Index

119